Last Wake Up Call

"A New Theory of the Revelations"

Published by Publishing House

The Presbyterian Church of Korea

Editor by Hyun Ju Lee
Book design by Hyun Jung Oh
Cover design by Seorosarang

Publisher Rev. Ro Won Park
Published by Publishing House of the Presbyterian Church of Korea

This book is printed on acid-free paper.
Printed in Korea

Last Wake up Call
ISBN 89-398-3430-5
1. New Testament Theology   2. Christian Ethics

Preface to the English Edition

"Jesus said also to the people, when you see the cloud coming up from the west, at once you say that it is going to rain-and it does. And when you feel the south wind blowing, you say that it is going to get hot-and it is. Hypocrites! You can look at the earth and sky and predict the weather, why, then, don't you know the meaning of this present times?"(Luke 12:54-56)

Jesus condemned the Teachers of Law, the Pharisees, even predicted their punishment by God in Matthew Chapter 23. If we do not know the meaning of the present times, Jesus would say, "You, hypocrites!"

We have seen the black clouds in the skies of the Middle East and strong winds begin to blow from the USA, to Afghanistan and toward to Iraq. We have to know the meanings of these present events. Why? What might be the meaning of these present events? For example,

The suicide Islam militant attack on New York and

Washington on September 11 2001.

Why did the United States start the War Against Terror in Afghanistan and seek to attack?

Why the serious conflict between Israel and Palestine?

Why is it so important to know the meaning of the present time? We should be sensitive regarding times because Christianity is the religion of time and history. When God created the universe, that was the beginning of time and history, and when Jesus comes back to us for the final judgment, that will be the end of time and history of the world.

Jesus began his redemptive task on the cross of Calvary some 2,000 years ago, and it will be accomplished on the day when he comes back to us. We should be sensitive to the times because we meed to be spiritually engaged with Jesus to be the fiancés when we accept Jesus in our heart, and will have the wedding ceremony that day when Jesus comes back to us. It would be normal for the fiancés to be sensitive for the wedding day, but if not sensitive that is abnormal. It is really fair and proper that the fiancés are sensitive for the wedding day. If we believe Jesus, his word, his promissory note in the Bible for the Second Advent and love him, we would be more than sensitive and sincerely long for the day.

How could we analyze the time? We have his love letter, the

Bible, there are the signs of his days ; Matt. 24, Mark 13, Luke 21, and particularly Revelation. Revelation is the spiritual clock the fiances must to know how to analyze the time.

When you finish to read this book, *Last Wake Up Call*, I would hope that you would answer all those questions which I raised in this paper. The purpose of this book is to help the readers to understand the fulfillment of the prophecies of Revelation in the history of the world. I would also hope to wake many believers up by this book.

Finally, I extend my appreciation to those who helped me to translate and revise this book ; Elder, Jae Kyung Kim, Miss, Hee Sook Song, and Mrs. Marian MacDanold.

I dedicate this book to Elder, Doo Nam Koh, My Father, a Martyr.

August 15, 2002
Billy Won Koh

Publiſhing the Enlarged Second Edition in Korean

The first edition was published as the title of *The Secret of the Seven Seals and World Mission* in 1995.

I praise the Lord, that the enlarged second edition is going to be published as *After Economic And Energy War* in this year.

Revelation is the only prophetic book in New Testament and prophesied the events which would be fulfilled in the last days. The prophecies of Revelation has been clearly fulfilled in last 10 years that I decided to publish the enlarged second edition to add more articles which have been fulfilled of the prophecies in Revelation.

Since 1800 A.D., the prophecy of Revelation has been rapidly fulfilled. The appearance of the white horse in 6:1-2, was the Western Colonial War. Through this white horse era the Gospel began to quickly spread out to all over the world by the wave of the Western Colonialists. The next horse was the red horse, which was the Communist Revolutionary Ideological War. As a result the Cold War Era was started by 1950, and the small and weak races and countries which were the colony of the Western powerful nations have been the newly emerged independent nations that ended the Western Colonial Era.

The third horse was the black horse which was the Economic War started by European Economic Union movement in 1950. As the result, the serious economic block war was started and new four blocks ; European Union, North America Free Trading Association, Asian +3, and ICM, are in the middle of the economic war. And USSR has collapsed and the Eastern Communist Nations become the democratic nations that the Communist Revolutionary War Era ended.

The final horse is the pale horse which is the Islam Revolutionary War or Energy War was begun in 1973 as result the Euphrates River War in Iraq will be broken out soon as the prophecy in Revelation 9:14-16 so that the economic war will be ended.

Oil has become a powerful weapon and the oil producing countries seems to control the world economy today.

We have seen the black clouds in the sky of the Middle East. I would hope the readers to be waken up by this book. I would hope to wake the readers up by this book in this critical time.

Nov. 11, 2000.
Billy Won Koh

8

Table of Contents

Chapter 1
The Introduction

In Old Testament, there are 16 prophetic books but in New Testament there is only one book, Revelation. The core of the prophecy in Old Testament is regarding the first coming of Jesus, and the New Testament is regarding the second of coming Jesus.

The study on the prophetic books, very difficult because it is study for the invisible future history. When we study the other books, four Gospels and Letters in the New Testament the interpretations seems to be very much similar, but Revelation there is very much diversity of the interpretations. For this reason, many scholars do not try to interpret it, even John Calvin did not from Chapter 4.

Revelation starts with seven letters and ends with many prophecies which are not sure the historical period:whether it is for the past, present or future history. To study Revelation, therefore, an expeditionary search some treasurer in deep sea. We need the wisdom of the Holy Spirit which the Text is also emphasis on that:

> "This calls for wisdom. Whoever is intelligent can figure out the meaning of the number of the beast, because the number stands for the name of someone. Its number is 666"(Rev. 13:18).
>
> "This calls for wisdom and understanding. / The seven heads are seven hills, on which the woman sits"(Rev. 17:9).

The Two Motivations to Study Revelation

In 1950 when I graduated from the Korean Presbyterian Theological Seminary the Student Graduating Committee suggested to the graduating class to pick up one of each books from the Bible and write a sermon from that book and we would continue to study on that book and if it is possible to write a professional books of each students. When I picked one book up that was Revelation.

The Graduation Gift of God

I believe that God gave me the Book of Revelation as a graduation gift and continued studying on this book, Revelation, in my whole life.

After graduating from the Seminary I was ordained as a Korean Presbyterian Minister at the age of 27. In 1955 I began to serve as a pastor and continue to read as many books on Revelation.

I am still studying it. However, it is and was very hard to figure out which interpretations were accurate of the book of Revelation among its numerous commentaries and books. It was my first motivation to study Revelation in my whole life.

A Theological Question on the Tribulation

I had one more motivation to study Revelation.

I had been fasting and praying for several days on the top of Samkak mountain near Seoul, Korea in the first week of August, 1957. At that time I was a young minister. I just begun to know the taste of the prayer, especially on the mountains. I had a serious theological question on the tribulations to God.

It was the end of Korean War. Most of the houses and building were destroyed by the War. People had to live in huts made of paper boards without protection from the cold. And over one million orphans on the streets became beggars, and more than 330,000 war widows without houses and food suffered from insomnia for their economic distress and crying out for their children in midnight. More than 5 million North Korean refugees came down to South for having the freedom without any food, houses, jobs and money. We could not see any hope of Korea in the future.

I was serving as the senior pastor at the Susanjang Church in Seoul, which was the war widows church. Rev. Dal Bin Chung, who was the Chief Army Chaplain in service of the Department of Defense, was the founder of this church and helping a lot to the war widows. We held the worship service in the auditorium of the Susanjang Factory that was built by the Department of Defense of Korea for war widows. The widows could work at the factory which make the clothing for the discharged solders. They worked all day long and leave their children at the factory nursery. They wept when we sing the hymns and listening my sermons. They lost their husbands and family members during the Korean War. Most of their age were average 26 years old. My heart was so painful and sad for thinking of that tribulation of our people.

And on the other hand the administration of the Liberal Party was so corrupted and cruel to the people in many ways. For example, the highway patrols use to ask money to the violated person instead of taking a ticket. They used the gang members for the political purpose and the head of gangs was a secretary of the President, whose name was Mr. Kwak Young Joo. So the gangsters were outrageous to the people. The most heartbreaking event which I saw was trying to demolish down the shacks made by the paper boards. And then people collected money to give the police men, and then they left. I couldn't see any hope for our nation.

During the Korean War, my self also fled from North Korea to South for the freedom, separated from my family by along. My father was killed by the Communist government in the North, became a martyr. I fled to South to continue the theological

Seminary education by self-supporting effort. I was suffering by the cirrhosis of the liver but no medicine that near by dead.

I began to arise a serious question, why? Why? Why? Oh God, on my people and me. I thought that God might have a reason even we do not know about. Because God told us "even one sparrow falls to the ground without your Father's Will." What might be God's will on this tribulation on me and my people? That's why I went up to top of the mountain for fasting prayer to know the will of God on my people.

The Providence of God On My People

It was 1 AM on August 8th ; I fell asleep falling down on the rock of the mountain. In a dream the Lord called me and I responded in great delight, "Here I am, Lord!" The Lord told me in his most merciful voice the following:

> "I am training your people including you by the tribulations to use your people as the great missionary power in the last days. You may call the 10,000 members Korean Church is not large church in Korea, and also thousands of Korean missionaries to all over the world. Open Revelation 7:1-3 and read it"

I awakened and hurried into my tent to light a candle and read Revelation 7:1-3. But I could not comprehend the meaning of the verse at all. Also it seems to me impossible. The largest church at that time was the Young Nak Presbyterian Church in Seoul, have around 2,000 members including kids and average attendance of Korean church on Sunday worship service was around 45 people. How could the Korean church be that much growing and sending the thousands of missionaries? But I believed that it would be possible if it is the will of God who would stop Him.

That dream is now reality as you know it. The largest protestant churches are in South Korea and over 10,000 Korean missionaries now all over the world. Praise the Lord! He is almighty and faithful.

To Agree the Futuristic Approach of the Interpretation

After 15 years of study on Revelation I drew a conclusion that the futuristic approach of the interpretation seemed to me very much appropriate. I have tried to read as many as books of the futuristic interpretation. But I was not satisfied with those interpretations in the commentaries and books so I began to study on my own. I have read Revelation at least 1,000 times since 1970s with prayer for the wisdom of the Holy Spirit to understand correctly the prophecies in Revelation until 1985.

At that year, I finally could see dimly the content of Revelations' prophecy. My conclusion was that if my interpretation is accurate then soon a serious event will happen in Iraq, where the Euphrates River is running. If some serious problem will be blackening at the Iraq, my interpretation would be accurate. Then I will write a book of Revelation.

As I had a premonition, Iraq invaded Kuwait on August 2, 1990, as a result the Gulf War was started by January 17, 1991 and ended by April 6, 1991. I had a confidence of my interpretation of the Revelation and since then began to write the manuscript for this Book, little by little every day during my ministry of the Youngnak Presbyterian Church in Atlanta Georgia.

Korean Edition was Published

1995, it was the 40th Anniversary of my ministry, the session of my church suggested me to publish a book in remembrance of the 40th Anniversary that I published the first edition on July 30, 1995, titled as "The Secret of the Seven Seals and World Mission." It was sold out 5,000 copies in three months in Korea, have to continue to print four more times.

The second edition was published on February 1, 2001 as the title, "After the Economic and Energy War" for adding some of the fulfillment of the prophecy in last 6 years. I translated the second edition from Korean to English for the publication.

Chapter 2
Diversity of Interpreting Revelations

The most difficult thing in studying Revelations is that each commentary has different views of interpretation. The interpretations of the Gospels and Letters in New Testament have almost similarities but it can not be found in the commentaries of Revelations. I found it to be quite difficult studying Revelations due to the large diversity in interpretations.

Revelations starts with a letter style first but it is a prophetic book that concludes with a prophecy. Revelation does not tell us the timings, whether it is for the historical event happening in the past, present or future. That is the reason there are so many diversities in the interpretations of Revelations.

It requires wisdom to study it like you were looking for treasures in the deep blue seas or probing out the answer to a great secret. That wisdom comes from the Holy Spirit, not from worldly wisdom. Revelation itself also recognizes it as the following verses:

"If anyone has insight, let him calculate the number of the beast, for it is man's number. His number is 666"(Rev. 13:8).

"This calls for the mind with wisdom. The seven heads are the seven hills on which the woman sits"(Rev. 17:9).

Interpreting the approaches of Revelation.

There are two approaches in the general interpretation of Revelation.

Interpretation Symbolic Way

It emphasizes that Revelation tells about the truth of Christianity symbolically rather than regarding it as the prophecies of historical events. It views the truth that Christianity will overcome any historical adversities or some theological truth as a work expressed symbolically. The doctoral faction that has such a viewpoint is as follows.

The School of Spiritual Interpretations

This Spiritual School opposes to interpret the passages of Revelation literally, and they regard it has a historical principal of man that is shown in a symbolic way. That is, it has presented the principal that the good will gair. victory in the end even though evil seems to win at first because God rules history. History is repeated by the challenge of evil, the response of good against it and the victory of good in the end. Revelation is considered to show that principle and is denied as a book of prophecy. Such opinion had many followers from the ancient Alexander School to the modern schools who consider the difficult passages of the Bible as expressions of parable style.

The School of Theological Interpretations

This school considers that Revelation is a myth and thinks it is a theological truth behind a symbolic myth. It is considered that Revelation has been recorded to have us believe the fact of God's absoluteness that no one can win against him. He controls and rules history. In his hands and will complete the final judgment at the degenerate age of unrighteousness and immorality, heresy and antichrist, injustice and corruption, pleasure-seeking and money worship which will rise like in the era of Noah. Its point of view is that Revelation is to show the theological truth of our achieving victory when we struggle against crisis or difficulties with faith of believing in his absoluteness.

The School of Literary Interpretation

This school believes that the book of Revelation is a literary work and that pieces of records have been edited by an unknown person trying to interpret it classifying into literature, comparative religion and its forms and style. This school has greatly influenced the interpretation of modern theology.

The School of Physiological Interpretation

This school tries to interpret Revelation physiologically looking at Revelation as a physiological phenomenon.

The above four schools all deny Revelation as a book of prophecy. Of course they recognize the teachings of theological thoughts, historical principals or Christian truths from this book. But if they try to interpret Revelation denying the fact of prophecy that Jesus had emphasized several times in the book, it would be far from the point of Jesus' intentions. Revelation is a book recorded by St. John when Jesus appeared to John and told him to write,

"what you have seen, what is now and what is going to happen in the future"(Rev. 1:19).

"What you have seen" means various visions that had been shown to John and "what is now and what is going to happen" means the historical events that will be accomplished in the future. The Book of Revelation is definitely prophecy. The Lord had clearly nailed that the record of this book was prophecy. Let's look at the following verses.

"Blessed is he who reads and those who hear the words of the prophecy and heeds the things which are written in it"(Rev. 1:3).

"And behold, I am coming quickly. Blessed is he who heeds the words of this book"(Rev. 22:7).

"Do not seal up the words of the prophecy of this book" (Rev. 22:10).

"I testify to everyone who hears the words of the prophecy of this book ; and if anyone adds to them, God shall add to him plagues which are written in this book ; and if anyone takes away from the words of the book of prophecy"(Rev. 22:18-19).

These scriptures written in this book emphasize that this book is a prophecy. Therefore, Revelation has to be interpreted as prophecies that will happen in the history of the world as historical events. It is not an adequate interpretation according to the above Scriptures if the historical concept is excluded.

When the weather forecaster announces rainfall preparation against it is made. It would be a clear misunderstanding if a certain person thought the weather forecast was merely informing them of weather principle such as sunny or rainy sometimes, meaning of course that the growing of crops well would be accomplished when it rained or a psychological phenomenon because the weather forecaster eagerly looked forward to it raining.

In the same way, it will accomplish the writing of the book when we study it as the prophecy that will happen in history. We are to affirm that the Lord Jesus controls history today by his invisible hand behind history whenever historical events occur, in glorifying him and believing it according to the will of the Lord when we interpret it focusing our attention on the fulfillment of the mission given by him with the hope of the restoration of the Kingdom of God after the judgment of Satan and his followers on the day of the last judgment.

Interpreting as Prophecies

The second method is to study it as a book of prophecy that

prophesied historical events which is to be achieved inevitability in a certain time of history. There are three categories of schools studying it with such a viewpoint. The prophecy of the book is to be accomplished certainly in history but there are three different answers to the question of when this will be accomplished.

The School of the Past

This school thinks that the prophecy has already been achieved in the past. It was interpreted at the standpoint of the prophecy that Christians who lived in the early churches era would achieve a triumph over their struggle with the Roman Empire. For example, the Scripture of chapters 2 to 3 indicate the worship of the emperor, chapters 4 to 11 indicate the struggle and jealousy between the Church and Judaism, chapters 13 to 19 indicate the things that happened in the time of the Roman Emperor Nero and Domitian, and chapters 21 to 22 indicate the things that had been accomplished already and also some of the future. This doctrine is supported widely, but has no uniformity due to the various interpretations between scholars.

Interpretation Classifying in History

The school regards the prophecy of Revelation as one that will be accomplished in history and their view point is that the book is a compact one of all the historical events that will happen from the early church period to the second coming of Jesus.

There are two different opinions between these schools. One

thinks it to be applied only to the history of salvation and the other thinks it applies to all of world history. There are different interpretations and extreme confusion within these schools because they concretely classify the whole of history into seven classifications. There are no unified interpretations which cause severe confusion by saying that the letters sent to the seven churches would only indicate certain churches in a certain time or the certain emperor of a specific nation.

The Prospective School

This school view is that most of the prophecy of the book is to be accomplished right before his second coming. The Prospective School of Interpretation view is based on Revelation 1:9. "What you have seen" is John's experience in chapter one. "What is now" is regarded as the letter sent to the seven churches and "what is going to happen later" is viewed as the events that will be accomplished right before Jesus' second coming and at the end of history.

Let's analyze the described three doctrines. Of course there is some reasoning in the view of all schools. But the interpretation of the past makes it worthless even to read Revelation because all prophecy had already been accomplished in the past. As a result, his second coming and the last judgment are denied. However, the book calls our attention to his imminent second coming and emphasizes its value to read. Therefore, the view of the past school is not considered to be an adequate interpretation.

And the second doctrine that interprets the prophecy of the book classifying it into seven periods of time has no unity between schools causing confusion, therefore, we don't know which doctrine to take. The confusion itself in the inadequacy of the doctrine and the unreasonableness in the interpretation that tries to set historical events and chronologically classifying it into seven periods of time. Therefore, the interpretation of the school of the past can not be an adequate one. After all, the view standpoint that the book prophesies things that will happen before and after his second coming is more Biblical and reasonable because the prophecy of the book emphasizes the end of the world. My study is also on the standpoint of the school of the future.

Two Opinions of the School of the Future

There are two standpoints between the school of the future.

First Standpoint

The Scripture of Rev. 4:1, "come up here" is viewed as a rapture of the church in the space and chapter 6 thereafter, as the period of ordeal. The proof of its view is presented by the fact that the word 'church' appears from chapters one to three and none thereafter.

Second Standpoint

The Scripture of "come up here" is viewed as the word

given to John himself and it does not mean a rapture of the church. Its standpoint of study is that all events occurring after chapter six is the prophecy that will happen right before His second coming. I consider the latter view and writing on its standpoint.

The Reason for Choosing the Latter

Revelation is apparently a prophecy of eschatological nature noticing the urgency for reading the prophesy extensively and the emphasis for Christians to read it widely(1:3). The prophecy after chapter 6 would indicate the prophecy of events that would happen after his second coming. Therefore, we need to have no interest in reading it because it indicates events that will happen after the rapture of Christians. If we had any concern or fear with the tribulation period, what else would help us except the encouraging words of faith, "be always on the watch, and pray that you may be able to stand before the son of man"(Luke 21:36). Would the Lord have instructed it to be written in the only prophetic book of the New Testament and urge us to read it if it was not that important a prophecy? My answer is definitely "no." I believe that it had been emphasized for us to read it because the Christians living in the eschatological era should know it as important words of prophecy.

Consideration of the Purpose
of the Eschatological Prophesy

When we analyze the prophecies in the Gospel, all of them are the signs of the Second Advent.

1. Phenomenon of nature:Natural disaster such as famines and earthquakes(Matthew 24:8, Mark 13:8, Luke 21:11).
2. Phenomenon of churches:The disorder by heresy and the anti-Christ(Matthew 5,11, Mark 13:56, Luke 21:8).
3. Phenomenon of persecution:The believers will be suffered by tribulation and persecution everywhere(Matthew 24:9, Mark 9:12, Luke 21:12).
4. Moral phenomenon:The prevalence of iniquity and sin due to moral corruption(Matthew 24:12, Mark 13:12, Luke 21:34).
5. World wars:The wars between nations against nations (Matthew. 24:6-7, Mark 7:8, Luke 21:9-10).
6. International phenomenon:The independence of Israel and small and weak nations(Luke 21:29-30).

All of those prophecies are the eschatological prophecies. The following Scripture clearly shows the purpose of them:

> "Be on the watch, and pray that you may be able to escape all that is about to happen, and that you may be able to stand before the Son of Man"(Luke 21:36-37).

> If he comes suddenly, do not let him find you sleeping. What I
> say to you, I say to everyone:"watch!"(Mark 13:36-37).
>
> "Therefore keep watch, because you do not know on what day the
> lord will come. But understand this:if the owner of the house had
> known at what time of night the thief was coming, he would have
> kept watch and would not have let his house be broken into. So
> you also must be ready, because the son of man will come at an
> hour when you do not expect him"(Matt. 24:42-44).

The purpose of the prophecy of Jesus is to awaken the believers
spiritually at the end of the history to have them accomplish their
task. Since the prophecy in Revelation is certainly about the end
of the history of the world it is appropriate to think that they
had been revealed for the same purpose as the prophecy in the
Gospel. If the prophecy of chapter 6, thereafter, was limited only
to the events of the great tribulation this book may not be
considered to be important because its purpose is not identical
and certain as the purpose of the prophecy in the Gospel. The
conclusion that the eschatological prophecy must accord with the
purpose of the Gospel is considered to be reasonable and
appropriate. Because the prophecy that will be accomplished in
history as signs of his second coming has the reason of helping
believers awake to achieve the victory in their missions.

The Relationship with the Eschatological
Prophecy of the Gospel

What is the mutual relationship of the prophecy in the book with the one in the Gospel? As the nature of the eschatological prophecy of the Gospel has been described earlier, both prophecies cannot be contrary or conflict with each other because the prophet is the same Jesus Christ. For example, the prophecy in the Scripture of this Gospel of the kingdom will be preached in the whole world as a testimony to all nations. And then the end will come (Matt. 24:14) by Jesus can not be said "end will come even before the Gospel spreads to all nations." Therefore, prophecies in Revelation are complementary to the one in the Gospel, supplementary to the prophecy of the Gospel or the prophecies in more detail and concrete. By the reason mentioned above, I am going to interpret Revelation from the standpoint that prophecies of signs of his second coming and great tribulation are described together in the prophecies after chapter six of Revelation.

Chapter 3
Introduction of Revelation(chapter 1-5)

Classification of Revelation

The book can be classified into three categories as follows ;

1. Introduction, Chapter 1-5
   A. John Encountered with Jesus, Chapter 1
   B. Letters Sent to Seven Churches, Chapter 2-3
   C. Saw the Throne of God.
2. Main Subject, Chapter 6-17
   A. Opened Seven Seals, Chapter 6 − 8:5
   B. Sounded Seven Trumpets, Chapter 8:6-10
   C. Interval Illustrations, Chapter 11-15
   D. Poured out Seven bowls, Chapter 16-17
3. Conclusion, Chapter 18-22
   A. Last Judgment, Chapter 18-20
   B. Kingdom of God, Chapter 21-22

As I have mentioned in the Introduction, I am trying to describe the interpretation for Seven Seals mainly that I want to write briefly the Introduction from Chapters 1-5, and the Conclusion from Chapters 18-22. But focus the main subject from Chapters 6-17. As it states in Rev. 1:9, Revelation has records of "what John has seen, what is now and what will take place later."

What John Has Seen

John wrote things that had been revealed to him at the exile on Patmos Island, during the persecuting reign of the Roman Emperor Domitian(A.D. 81-96). The Emperor Domitian along with Nero was anti-Christ and atrocious emperors who had intensively persecuted the early Christian Church. He had confiscated Christian's all properties, forced to be killed by fierce beasts in the Coliseum and sent distinguished persons into exile, among whom John was one of them.

On a Lord's Day John saw Jesus in a vision who was walking through seven lamp stands holding seven jars when John was praying earnestly for churches in Asia(presently Turkey) which were wandering without any shepherds in persecution. The Lord wore a golden sash around his chest like a king, his hair was white like wool showing his purity, his eyes were like blazing fire penetrating into person's heart, his feet were like bronze glowing in a furnace symbolizing judgement. In his right hand he held seven stars symbolizing the ministers. Out of his mouth came a sharp double-edged sword and his face was like the sun shining in all its brilliance. The Lord was protecting churches in severe persecution which were purchased at the cost of his blood while holding seven stars, symbolizing the ministers of whole world and walking through seven lamps stands, symbolizing all churches in the world. When John saw him, he fell at his feet as though he was dead, overwhelmed by his intensive purity, glory and dignity. But the Lord who won over death and darkness placed his right hand on John and said, "write what you have seen, what is now and what will take place later." Accordingly, John began to write Revelation.

Jesus Who Transcends Time

In the part of the Introduction the Lord emphasized two important things to John. First, it was emphasized that the Lord is the beginning, ongoingness and conclusion of history. The Lord said to John:

"Who is, and who was, and who is to come"(Rev. 1:4).
"I am the alpha and the omega who is, and who was, and who is to come"(Rev. 1:8).
"I am the first and the last"(Rev. 1:7).

Above Scriptures declare that the Lord who existed in the past is existing presently and will exist in the future, is the one to transcend time. As St. Augustine mentioned regarding time, his confession that to us the past does not exist because it is already gone but exists only in our memory as past events. The second World War was over and now we have peaceful era but the Japanese attack on Pearl Harbor with the second World War is remained as our memory at present time.

Our present is a moment, passing away. As soon as it is declared that present time is 40 seconds after ten of one P.M. On February 12th 1995, that time has passed away and does not exist at present. Therefore, the present is a passing moment that does not exist at present as geometry does not admit area of a dot.

The future does not exist at the present time because it has not come yet. Tomorrow does not exist at the present time because tomorrow is not here yet. The future exists only in our hope and expectation.

However, the past, present, and future are all present to the Lord because He is eternity. It is impossible for us to understand eternity because it is beyond our experience. But the Lord declared that He is eternal by His words,:"who is, and who was, and who is to come."

There have been many people recognize Jesus only as a historical person. The cause of persecution to early churches was because He proved Himself a Son of eternal God by the resurrection. He is really the one who has overcome even death. If the believers of the early churches did not have the firm faith of sharing in his death and resurrection how could they gain victory with the spirit of martyr over such cruel persecution and tribulation? Revelation of Jesus as the one who can transcend time might have given them strength and courage in the persecution. Stephen's face was like the face of an angel when he died a martyr because Christian's death is ultimately a step toward the eternal life. We have crossed over from death to life and possess eternity by being grafted into an eternal Jesus through our faith given by his Grace ; otherwise we are mortal beings in time. We are not to fear death because we have been prearranged to possess eternity.

The Focus of God's Providence

The Lord who was revealed to John appeared as the one who was walking between seven golden lamp-stands that symbolize whole churches in the world and seven stars that symbolize the servant of God in the world. Therefore, scholars who study Revelation insist that the prophecy of the book is limited only to the prophecy of events that will happen to the churches in the world. How could the prophecy of Jesus be limited only to churches when he is coming as a Chief Judge to judge the world?

It indicates that God's providence is focused to the churches of Jesus. Let's look at the Old Testament for example. We can notice that God ruled Israel as primary history in the world, although many nations were in the world. Therefore, Israel had a sense of superiority as a chosen people which led to the advocate of nationalism. What was the reason that God had ruled history of Old Testament era with deeper concern for Israel than gentiles?

Israel was such as a seedbed. A farmer prepares a rice seedbed first at the corner of his farmland when he tries to do rice farming in his entire rice paddy, and his main concern is concentrated with the seedbed by watering, fertilizing and weeding until they grow up. People who are not familiar with the farming may think that the farmer was trying to grow rice only at the corner of the paddy field. But the real plan of the farmer was to make a seedbed in order to cultivate entire rice paddy. Israel was a seedbed of the Old Testament.

The focal point of the providence of God is the redemptive history, the history of his Church. His Church is the seed of the Kingdom of God, and the seedbed. As the existence and the commission of Israel was so important in the Old Testament age, the existence and the commission of his Church which is his body is very important in New Testament age.

Revelation is emphasizing what kind of stance and commission of the church would take when the signs of the Second Advent will be fulfilled. We would invest all of our treasure:mind, time, talent, knowledge, money, gift, even life such as the pearl merchant(Matt. 13:45-46) for the commission of the last days.

Many historians insist that the reason of the raising and fall of the nations would be whether they could have the strong army or not, but Babylon and Red Army of Soviet had very strong army but fell. The communist emphasized the importance of the ideology that educated from the kids in the kindergarten and let all people get the armament of the communist ideology. They thought that the ideology is the key for raising and fall of any nations, but fell. Dr. Paul Kennedy wrote a book, "The Raising and Fall of the Great Nations" tried to insist the economical power is the key reason for the raising and fall of any nations. But Babylon and Sodom had enough economic power and fell.

Of course all of those may be a part of the reason but main reason is the moral corruption that God judge them. The history of the world began by God, and the end of the history will be by God. He rules the past, present and future of history. The history of the world seems to progress by world leaders, G8, but by the hand of God in behind of a curtain that will be proved by this book.

Chapter 4
The Letters to Seven Churches

The Seven Churches in Revelation actually existed in Asia Minor. At that time, they were believed to have a connection with the disciple John. These letters should be understood as a message not only for the seven churches, but also for all the churches in the world. Because the message contains eschatological prophecy which alarms urgently his churches in the modern era. Since many good commentaries and similar interpretation regarding these letters had been published I will, therefore, just summarize the significant points here. When we analyze the contents of letters to seven churches we find that they are closely related to the Lord Jesus' eschatological prophecy in the Gospel. The following explains the emphasis made in each letter.

To the Ephesus Church-Revelation 2:1-7

The letter to the church in Ephesus emphasizes to recover "your first love that you have forsaken"-Revelation 2:3-4. Jesus predicts the same condition in the last days, "because of the increase of wickedness, the love of most will grow cold"(Matthew 24:12). It means that extreme selfishness among people will be one of the signs of the last days. After Jesus' prophecy he stresses the preparation for the end in three parables of Matthew chapter 25. He predicts the severe coldness of human society in the last days through parable about a lamb and a goat.

"For I was hungry and you gave me nothing to eat, I was thirsty and you gave me nothing to drink, I was a stranger and you did not invite me in, I needed clothes and you did not clothe me, I was sick and in prison and you did not look after me" (Matthew 25:42-43).

Jesus asks the Christians to recover their first love in order to cope with the apocalyptic condition of the times. He is concerned about the Christians if they rather get tainted by the trend of the world than practice love of the Lord.

What is Meant by the First Love?

Remember when we first experience the amazing love of Jesus we confess all our sins to the Lord, We're so moved by his Love, filled with thankfulness, and devote ourselves freely to the Lord. We're delighted to praise and worship the glory of the Lord and read the Bible all night by being rapt in his word. We were eager to testify about Jesus' love while feeling compassion for lost souls. We throw away all worldly values like garbages out of gratefulness of becoming God's children by our faith in Jesus Christ. We decided to obey God's word and to march against all the difficulties and trials for the joy and glory of his eternal inheritance in heaven. Thus, our first love means our confession that but the drops of grief can never repay the debt of love I owe. Here Lord, I give myself away ; this all that I can do for you.

How to Recover our First Love?

We fail to keep our first love in many times. However, we can recover this love because the Lord never asks us anything impossible. Then how?

First, we have to remember the height from which you have fallen-Revelation 2:5. Ask yourself why you have forsaken your first love. Is it because of a desire for materialism, ambition, lust, and hatred or envy? Or is it because you can't forgive someone? If you love something more than obeying the Lord's word, it is the height from which you have fallen. When you find the height you should repent. You have to throw away what you have against someone, forgive someone, pay off the debts like Zacchaeus, and repent with tears, kneel down before the Lord. Easy to fall but hard to recover. However, if you repent hard the Lord will forgive you and the Holy Spirit will help you recover your first love. Pray in over night, fasting, and unisonous prayer will shorten its recovery time.

The Source of Strength

When we recover the first love the strength works through this love. The source of strength which makes us overcome our egoism, the worldly life, Satan and trials is hidden in this love. 1 Corinthians chapter 13 expresses that all our good deeds are nothing if we do not have this love. Nothing means things like a weed, a husk or a fruitless tree to be burn out. The apostle Paul compared Christian life without love to build a house with logs, weeds, and hay. When God judge them, loose everything. But if we build a house with the most precious stones, we will get the glorious prizes (1 Cor. 3:10-15).

To the Smyrna Church-Revelation 2:8-11

The main point of the letter to the Church in Smyrna, is not to be afraid of any suffering and trials but to be faithful, even to be killed. The period of the early Christian churches has been called the period of persecution due to the severe persecution by Roman emperors. The Lord foretells that the churches in the last days will also experience the same.

"But before all this, they will lay hands on you and persecute you. They will deliver you to synagogues and prisons, and you will be brought before kings and governors, and all on account of my name"(Luke 21:12).

"Then you will be handed over to be persecuted and put to death, and you will be hated by all nations because of me" (Matthew 24:9).

"Because those will be days of distress unequaled from the beginning, when God created the world, until now-and never to be equaled again"(Mark 13:19).

Thus, these eschatological prophecies emphasize that there will be days of severe suffering in the end of history. The prophecy of the suffering here must not be interpreted to be the great tribulation. If so, the return of Jesus must be followed after the tribulation and this prophecy also includes all the Christians, who will be lifted up to heaven(rapture).

Some analysts of the scriptures make mistakes by interpreting that the Christians have almost nothing to do with the tribulation, which leads the Christians not to be prepared. In Christianity many have experienced severe suffering and many died as the martyrs in the early Christian Church era. After the Reformation people were persecuted by the Catholic Church for following the Reformed Christian tradition in many places. Since 1800 the Gospel has been spread all over the world by the strong missionary movement despite the suffering and persecution. Since 1917 severe persecution has been ongoing in the communist regime and Islamic countries even now. During the period of the early Christians in the catacombs could escape the persecution, but under the modern communist regime even underground churches like in the catacombs can not exist due to this continuing intense persecution. We should prepare ourselves for tribulation because the return of Jesus Christ is near. We need to have the faith of the martyrs, even this kind of faith does not happen in a day. It requires us to train ourselves by obeying the Lord's word at the risk of our lives in everyday life.

To the Pergamun Church-Revelation 2:12-17

The particular lesson for the church in Pergamum is not to hold to the teaching of Balaam, the false prophet. According to Jesus, "many will come in my name, claiming 'I am he,' and will deceive many"(Mark 13:6).

"For false Christ and false prophets will appear and perform great signs and miracles to deceive even the elect-if that were possible"(Matthew 24:24).

Jesus predicts there will be an enormous confusion in Christian churches with the appearance of false prophets, heresies, and cult, which indicates another sign of the first days. Jesus told us this word because we need to stand on the truth and fight against the heresy.

Heresy has been an influential problem since the early church period and became more powerful since the 18 century. In particular, Korean churches after the Korean War have experienced several serious heretical problems, such as the Unification Church by Sun-myung Moon and the Chondohwan by Tae-sun Park. Even today, heresy disguises itself in public as a normal church or a religious body which created a huge confusion and challenge to the existing Christian churches. Its seriousness became extreme when Mr. Myung-hwan Tahk, who examined the problem of heresy and cult in depth, was murdered by a heretic terrorist.

Most of the heresy and cult confusing Korean religious circle had a tendency of mysticism. Therefore, we must teach people that the foundation of faith is not human experience or reason, but the Bible, the only word revealed by God. To protect ourselves from falling for the heresy we need to stay well informed about it. We have seen so many people harmed by heresy and cults. Some ruined both his/her family after joining the heretic movement by Tae-sun Park. Some families closed their business, stopped their children from studying, sold all the possessions and contributed them to a cult claiming the return of Jesus on October 28, 1992.

In fact, existing churches should take the responsibility because they neglected teaching people the truth of the Bible correctly. We should stay alert not to fall for the heresy and cult while remembering the Jesus' warnings as well as standing on His word.

To the Thyatira Church-Revelation 2:18-29

The warning to the church in Thyatira is to repent of adultery and sexual immorality.

"Be careful, or your hearts will be weighed down with dissipation, drunkenness and the anxieties of life, and that day will close on you unexpectedly like a trap"(Mark 21:34).

One of the signs in the last days is that people fall into the trend of sexual immorality. Think about our generation. Our teenagers are imbued with the idea of free sex which cause teen-pregnancy to become a social problem. With a growing divorce rate children are wandering the streets to resist against their parents. These kids mostly end up with drugs or crimes, which became a serious social problem in the US. Historians say that the fall of a nation or generation had a close relation with its sexual and ethical corruption, and homosexuality sets an extreme example. Some years ago at Sunset Boulevard in Los Angeles there was a huge protest by 10,000 homosexuals demanding their marriage to be legally permitted. President Clinton approved the military service of homosexuals and some denomination in US approved the ordination of the homosexual minister and some denominations have been having discussions on the matter of ordaining the homosexual minister for many years. When a generation becomes corrupted like this, even Christians are easy to be contaminated. We have to protect the young generation of our days from contamination and equip them with the Lord's word and the Holy Spirit to grow to be pure Christian.

To the Sardis Church-Revelation 3:1-6

The Lord asks the Christians in the Sardis Church to reach out and keep their faith firmly. He spoke in parables about the end as follows:

> "The bridegroom was a long time in coming, and they all became drowsy and fell a sleep"(Matt 25:5).

"But suppose that servant is wicked and says to himself 'my master is staying away a long time'"(Matthew 24:48).

Jesus warns that there will be many spiritually dormant believers in the last days. Why our spirit gets dormant? It is like the times of Noah because all the people experience darkness like a night, caused by the Mormonism, hedonism, and dissipation. Even Christians become spiritually relaxed and dormant, as Jesus said, "you have reputation of being alive, but you are dead" (Revelation 3:1). That is, he warns there will be many believers for the form's sake, even inside of the church.

In order to keep our spirit awake, we need an empirical information concerning what is being dormant or awake like. How can we recognize our spiritual status if we do not examine them? Based on the results of this study, we can realize that our spirit is dormant and try to wake it up. Of course, differences in individual experiences are possible, but I'd like to focus on some identical characters showing that our spirit is dormant. According to my study, I found that following characters appear when my spirit is dormant.

1. The peace and joy of my heart disappear, but the complexity, anxiety and fear resides in me.
2. Experience difficulty in praying, and the praying time gets shorter and powerless.
3. Lose the joy of spiritually deep understanding when reading

the Bible. Read the Bible just to prepare for the sermon and Bible study.

4. The self-love fills my heart, so the love for church, the Body of Christ weakens.

5. Forget the thankfulness for the Lord and his mercy.

6. Forget the love toward other souls, and be indifferent to the missionary work.

7. Be lost in the battle against Satan because of my weak spiritual strength.

8. Forget the glory of the cross, and avoid suffering for the Lord.

Staying awake is what Jesus emphasized most in his eschatological prophecy.

Refer to the following words:Matthew 24:42-43, 25:13, Mark 13:33, 35, and 37, Luke 21:36

Jesus repeats, "therefore keep watch", as the conclusion of his prophecy about the last days. How can we be awake to watch? There must be a reason when our spirit gets dormant, so we must find the reason and repent it.

"The night is nearly over ; the day is almost here. So let us put aside the deeds of darkness and put on the armor of light. Let us behave decently, as in the daytime, not in orgies and drunkenness, not in sexual immorality and debauchery, not in dissension and jealousy. Rather, clothe yourselves with the Lord, Jesus, Christ, and do not think about how to gratify the desires of the sinful nature"(Roman 13:12-14).

To the Philadelphia Church-Revelation 3:7-13

The Philadelphia Church received only the praise without any reproach. This church sets an example which Jesus wants us to be in the last days. Jesus praised particularly two points of this church. First, with little strength yet it has kept his word and has not denied His name. Second, since it has kept his command to endure patiently he will also keep it from the hour of trial and no one will take its crown.

Keeping His Word With Little Strength

This strength came from the faith, so it is God's strength. When we obey the Lord's command with little faith, this strength keeps growing. When the widow at Zarephath obeyed with a handful of flour and a little oil this obedience returned to solve her food problem during the three and half years of drought. When David obeyed with five small stones he killed Goliath and Israel won a great victory. When Andrew obeyed with five loaves of bread and two fish Jesus fed five thousand people with them and twelve baskets of broken pieces were left over.

One cannot be a great Christian overnight. Rather, one should practice daily to learn how to obey the Lord little by little and step by step. It's just like one cannot be a world-renowned pianist overnight. It takes training and practice daily with devotion. One also should train oneself to be godly everyday.

It is impossible to have the faith of a martyr in one day. One needs to start learning from the basics, such as daily prayer with reading the Bible, keeping the Sabbath, and giving the Tithe. One's daily little obedience keeps his/her faith growing and as faith grows the strength also automatically grows.

Keeping His Command to Endure Patiently

It is not easy to keep the command of God to endure patiently. It requires us to know the worth of the cross, to have a faith of loving the cross, and to see the glory of future with eyes of spirit. Job overcame the difficult trials with the faith confessing his every possession belongs to God. Daniel trusted that the almighty God is always with him which saved him from the lions' den. Paul had a faith knowing that his present sufferings are not worth comparing with the glory that will be revealed in him which enabled him to walk through the road of difficulties with joy. We need the training to keep the command of God to endure patiently to overcome the diverse difficulties in this last days.

To the Laodicea Church-Revelation 3:14-22

Jesus asks the Laodicea Church to repent its being lukewarm. It predicts there will be many formal Christians in last days.

"When the Son of man comes, will He find faith on the earth?" (Luke 18:8)

What Does it Mean to be Lukewarm?

To be lukewarm means to be neither hot nor cold. Being hot means having faith, and being cold no faith. Faith is fundamentally hot because it is God's gift consisting of the hot love of God, the hot blood of Jesus, and the hot fire of the Holy Spirit. A faithful Christian must be hot when they pray, praise, and love other souls. When God's hot love fills them up their life also get hot with God's love.

Being lukewarm indicates people leading a formal Christian life that is neither faithful nor faithless. They enjoy in the worship at the church, not practice the Word of God, but they enjoy a sinful life like non-Christians outside the church. They do not give up drinking, smoking, fighting and being dissipated, jealous, and lewd. However, they attend the service on Sundays. They attend to the Sunday worship service with the godly Christian, but live social life just like a non-Christians.

The Condition of the Lukewarm Christians

Jesus describes the lukewarm Christians as wretched, pitiful, and poor, which expresses their spiritual poverty. This poverty led them to be wretched and pitiful.

Then what is the reason of spiritual poverty?

"I counsel you to buy from me gold refined in the fire, so you become rich." According to Revelation 3:18, we became poor because we do not have this spiritual gold. Then what is the spiritual gold refined in the fire? These have come so that your faith − of greater worth that gold, which perishes even though refined by fire···−1 Peter 1:7 also indicates that this poverty means spiritual one, not material.

This spiritual hunger must be caused by not taking spiritual bread and not drinking spiritual water. As the Israelites were provided with Manna and water during their travel in the desert we need spiritual bread everyday while living in the world like the assembly in the desert(Acts 7:38). Korean church is young with only little over one hundred years of history. However, it became the most powerfully growing church in the world. I believe the most significant reason must be the daily early morning prayer meeting every day, which provided the Korean church with spiritual bread. In addition, recent enthusiastic movements, such as the Bible study and lay men training through discipleship play important roles in providing spiritual bread. Therefore, these movements are powerful and have influences on the growth of church. It is natural for the churches leading these movements to experience the spiritual awakening. The provision of spiritual bread has the Christian avoid hunger and brings new life to the Christians. We also notice the American churches, which experience a repaired growth, have small groups for the cell Bible study.

They Did Not Realize to be Naked

If someone does not realize his nakedness, it means he leads a shameful life without knowing it as a shame. Who is the one in this spiritual condition?

1. He is tormented by the guilty conscience, but does not repent

The human conscience means that we are superior to animals. We do not know where is our conscience. Philosopher Immanuel Kant regarded the conscience as a kind of rational function by calling it 'practical reason.' He probably thought conscience is located in head. However, many people think conscience is in heart, but nobody proved the exact address of conscience. This mystical conscience proves the fact that human beings have one more thing than animals. I believe that conscience is a function of spirit. Philosophers call this spirit as being or existence, but Bible calls as the spirit. Whatever the name is, it means human beings have one more thing than animals.

A man does not listen to the voice from his conscience, which makes him realize the human value, it degrades him to an animal. Moreover, it is more tragic if a man does not repent, even though he hears the voice. Particularly, even after the spiritual born-again experience if he does not repent in hearing the voice it is truly like walking around naked. Confession of sin and repentance move the heart of God. Whatever sins we committed God will cleanse it white and clothe us with fine linen. If we keep disobeying the voice of conscience we become insensible to immorality. So we may commit shameful sins without being tormented by guilty conscience. This serious condition is described in the Bible to be hypocritical liars whose consciences have been seared as with a hot iron.

2. He does not repent after hearing the word of God

When we pray, read the Bible, listen to sermon or Bible study hour, God speaks through the inspiration and the word. Whoever joins church activities after born-again experience can hear God's voice. This Word is active and penetrates to dividing soul and spirit, joints and marrow. This voice is the Word of God, that we should obey but if one disobeys and lives on his own will he is spiritually naked. When we hear sermon we should try to listen to what God wants to say to us and as soon as we hear God's voice we must obey right away.

3. Public opinion is the second conscience

Public opinion is the second conscience. Of course, sometimes public opinion can be distorted for the political purpose. However, most public opinion is correct(70-75%) in terms of statistics. So advanced democratic countries conducts a survey and announces the result whenever an important issue rises. "It is interesting to see the note of approximately 2-3% of error may be possible", which is written following the public survey statistics on newspapers.

It is helpful to listen carefully to the public opinion. It is because God also works through the public opinion. We have witnessed so many tragic incidents in Korean history caused by ignoring the public opinions.

For example, we remember the tragic end of the administration of the Liberty Party in 1950-1960s who did not listen to the public opinion about a Constitutional amendment. They passed the amendment by rounding off to the nearest integer, which left a shameful stain on Korean history of Constitutional administration. At last, this incident caused the Revolution on the 19 of April, 1960 and many young people were shot to death and President Seung-man Lee, who devoted his whole life for the independence of Korea from Japan had to resign and end up his life alone while taking refuge in Hawaii, We should understand that the public opinion is the second conscience and its voice is connected to the voice of God.

We also clearly remember the tragic end of President Jung-Hee Park who passed the constitution for revitalizing reform by force. If he had respected the public opinion and had kept his public pledge of revolution, he would have had been a great man in Korean history.

If we do not learn the lessons from these past incidents in history and ignore the public opinion about ourselves we cannot get out of the shame as a naked man. The confession and repent of sin is the only way to be forgiven and cover our shameful nakedness.

4. They did not realize the blindness

The blind can not distinguish beauty or ugliness, valuable or valueless. Valuables are beautiful. A golden ring is more beautiful than a copper ring and a diamond ring is more beautiful than a gold ring. Gold is more expensive than copper and diamond is more expensive than gold. Beauty is directly proportional to value. Living a beautiful life means a valuable life. Therefore, one with sight means person with capability of discerning true value.

Once Russia sold Alaska to US without knowing its value, and a French Emperor also sold off a huge land in Central America. Judas Iscariot handed over Jesus for thirty silver coins without knowing his value.

A man builds his life on the foundation of his judgement of value. If one thinks money is the most valuable he does even unlawful things, such as fraud, theft, tax dodging, and drug selling, and some people end up in jail or capital punishment. If one judges power is the best he tries to take power by employing every possible form of tactics, such as deceitful public pledges, a rigged election, and even a coup d'etat, and once in power he does whatever to keep it.

Since a man builds his life on the foundation of his judgement of value true believers should make a right judgement of values with open eyes of the spirit. Things in the world we can see are valuable only during our lifetime but the spiritual things have eternal values. Our body also has its value while we are alive and turn into dust after death. However, our spirit lasts forever.

Once I was confronted by death at the age of 29 because of cirrhosis of the liver. One day I thought I might not see the sun rise of tomorrow again so I had my last prayer under a tent on Mt. Samkak. That night in a dream a person came to me and asked following questions, "What do you need? Money? Doctoral degree? Power? Or a beautiful woman to be your wife? Ask me. I will give you all you want." However, I did not need such things when I faced death. I said, "I don't need any money, power, a degree, or a woman." He said, "Then, what do you need?" When the person asked me again I pondered deeply and realized nothing I needed, but only the Lord Jesus who would lead me to Father's house after my death.

I found a true value at that night, just like a merchant who found a pearl. And I praised the Lord with the following song.

> I'd rather have Jesus than silver or gold ;
> I'd rather be his than have riches untold ;
> I'd rather have Jesus than houses or lands.
> I'd rather be led by his nail-pierced hand
> Than to be the king of a vast domain,
> or be held in sin's dread sway
> I'd rather have Jesus than anything
> this world affords today.

5. How to be hot

"Here I am! I stand at the door and knock. If anyone hears my voice and opens the door, I will come in and eat with him, and he with me"(revelation 3:20).

This Scripture show us how to be hot. We can not be hot by ourselves. But when the Lord come into our heart, that is, when he holds the Lordship and Kingship and works in us could be hot. It is because he is full of love and hot. His heart is filled with love of cross. If we respect his Lordship and Kingship and obey his command, he will control and take charge of our heart.

When his love fills us, we will be able to serve the Lord again with a hot heart. Only if we repent and open our heart to the Lord, he will change us to be hot.

Chapter 5
The Worship in Heaven

In chapter 4 and 5 the disciple, John, witnesses and describes worship before the throne in heaven. This form of worship is the original and model for the worship in churches on earth. The arrangement of sitting in the sanctuary ;

The Throne in Heaven is Located in the Center

This shows God is the center of our worship as well as the subject

The sanctuary in Catholic Churches displays the paintings or sculpture of Mary and the saints in front. That is why the Reformists got rid of these ornaments in the sanctuary to serve God to be the center of worship.

When we look at the sanctuary in most of the Reformed churches the cross and the Bible are in the center and sometimes two candles are located on their sides. Of course, they symbolize that the word of God and the cross of Jesus are the core of worship. However, modern churches put emphasis on the man and sometimes the grandeur of stained glass or the pipe organ behind the pulpit look like the center, displaying the wealth of the church. We must decorate the sanctuary of how to present God as the core of worship.

Then, how possibly can we decorate our sanctuary to show the character of God who sat on the throne? The one who sat on the throne is pure and holy like Jasper, balanced between justice and love like carnelian, and keeps his promises like a rainbow. How can we show these characters of God symbolically in the center of pulpit?

However, even though we are able to decorate the sanctuary like that it will be no use for hearts do not worship God as the core of our service.

Twenty-four elders' thrones

As I mentioned earlier in the Introduction, the number 12 is the symbol of the choice of God. The 12 elders who represent the chosen saints from the Old Testament church, and the other 12 elders are for the New Testament church are sitting surrounding the throne.

This symbolizes that all the saints who were saved in the Old and New Testaments ages will worship the Lord in the presence of God who sits in the center.

Christians should maintain their life as we worship God every moment as well as the time of worship service,

"Offer your bodies a living sacrifices, holy and pleasing to God this is your spiritual act of worship"(Romans 12:1).

This means our daily life should be the act of worship which means we should expose the world to the fragrance of Christ in our daily life and live to fulfill the great commission of light and salt like a letter from Christ. This also means that we are not Christians during service but recognize that our body is the temple setting goals for His glory and fulfilling the mission.

One of the problems of modern church is the fact that there are too many Christians only inside the church. They are Christians during service but live like non-Christians in their social life. As a result, it means a serious problem that there are not many changes in society in spite of the increase of Christians.

If the church does not work like light and salt of the world, then what the reason of the existence of church will be? If the solemnity and piety rule over our daily life, the social changes must follow and Christians will not be shunned by others. Once President Young-Sam Kim pointed out this problem at Presidential Prayer meeting on his inauguration day.

"Churches should fight against the social crime and corruption, but today's churches are rather contaminated by the corruption. Now is not late than never, churches should try to get rid of injustice and corruption by fulfilling the mission of light and salt of the world."

As 24 elders were seated before God all the time the saints

should always live like a worshipper.

The four living creatures before the throne

These four creatures were like a lion, an ox, a man, and an eagle. Prophet Isaiah also saw almost same vision and it is recorded in Isaiah 6:2 as seraphs instead of creatures. These spiritual beings, like angels, work to serve God in presence of his throne. Isaiah saw them each has six wings.

With two wings they covered their faces in sign of their respect for God, with two feet in sign of their humble service, and with two they were flying in sign of their loyal work.

The spiritual beings give glory, honor and thanks to God who sits on the throne and praise day and night:

"Holy, holy, holy is the Lord God almighty, who was, and is, and is to come"(Rev. 4:8-9).

The spiritual beings symbolize the work of the servants of God front of the throne of God. The Lord's servants at work must be intrepid like a lion to fight against the Satan, loyal like an ox to spread the Gospel, wise like a man to deal with this world, and improve themselves daily as an eagle flies high to the sky to build solid spiritual living.

The true meaning of worship is serving God and it should be like that of seraphs.

The status of the angel and the heavenly host

"Many angels, numbering thousands upon thousands, and ten

thousand times ten thousands"(Rev. 5:11).

This record shows a great company of the angel and the heavenly host is praising and singing, surrounding the throne. The responsibility of the angels is to praise God and help the work for His Kingdom.

Sometimes, the angels deliver joyous news to the people on earth(Luke 1:26-38), praise the glory of God with the heavenly host(Luke 2:13-14), and fight for the people of God with the host of heaven(Daniel 10:21, 2 kings 6:13-19). They are servants of God for his Kingdom.

We must carry out the work of sewing and worshiping the Lord in the status of the angel and the heavenly host at his church on earth. We should completely obey to God's will and word, serve and praise him often, and fight well against the influence of Satan.

Thus, according to the analysis of the arrangement of the sanctuary in heaven, we find that there is God's throne in the center, 24 elders' thrones around God's, four seraphs serve front of the throne, and an uncountable number of angels and heavenly host worship God surrounding His throne.

The Program of Service

The program of service is consisted of seven very simple procedures

1. Four spiritual creatures opened the service by singing the glory of God(Rev. 4:8-9).
2. Twenty-four elders worshiped God(4:10-11), took off the crown and praise.
3. An angel proclaimed the Word of God(5:1-2). There were answer to the Word and determination of action(5:5-7).
4. Twenty-four elders fell down with a harp and golden bowls full of incense(5:8).
5. Elders response(5:11-12).
6. Every creature in heaven and on earth and under the earth and on the sea, and all that is in them, singing in response(5:13).
7. Four living creatures closed the service by singing amen song (5:14).

In analyzing the program of the grand service in heaven it is very interesting to find it has five major components of the service at modern church. The five components are praise, prayer, scripture reading, offering, and sermon. In the book of Revelation these all five components are appeared, and the program of modern churches' service must have found its example after the study of Revelation by reformative predecessors.

According to the analysis of the service in heaven, the service began with the praise of "holy, holy, holy…" Next, twenty-four elders fell down and took off their crowns with praise and worship, which conforms to our confession of faith, praise and offering. Then, an angel delivered the message of God, which is today's sermon. Angels, heavenly hosts and all creatures' responding songs were followed. The service was ended by amen song by four living creatures.

I realized several important facts while studying the service in heaven recorded in Revelation.

A) I was deeply impressed by the scene that twenty-four elders took off their crowns and worshiped God by giving them front of His throne. The salvation is by the grace of God, but the crown is the prize of our deeds. Twenty-four elders' act shows that this prize is not for our meritorious deeds. "Even the precious prize belongs to the Lord, because He let the Holy Spirit inspire and work in us to obey him." Their attitude to the Lord inspires us what a worshiper should be like.

B) Action was followed immediately after delivering the message from God by a mighty angel, "who is worthy to break the seals and open the scroll?"(Rev. 5:2)

When John heard this he wept because no one was found who was worthy to open the scroll. Then one of the elders said to him, "do not weep! See, the lion of the tribe of Judah, the root of David, has triumphed. He is able to open the scroll and its seven seals." – 5:5

With this positive response, the Lamb, Jesus Christ came and took the scroll from the right hand of God. – 5:7

Thus, the church on earth should take a positive, obedient

action responding to the word of God proclaimed at the time of service. A pastor's sermon should not be one-sided delivery. It should lead the resolution of obedience from believers. I believe there must be a time of resolution for believers after the sermon and before the prayer by preacher.

C) Responding songs were followed. When the Lamb had taken the scroll the four living creatures and twenty-four elders praised Him with prayers and a new song and innumerable angels sang in response. − 5:11-13

In general, a choir sings after the prayer during the service but there is no responding song to the choir, which is different from the service in heaven. Therefore, I added two programs to the service after my study of Revelation. One is having a time of resolution after sermon. Our church members are encouraged to promise the obedience to today's message and leave the sanctuary. Another is that all the members stand up and sing in response to the choir's praise.

The Reason Why the Christians are not Present

Why there is no saint singing and worship at the service in heaven, along with seven spirits(holy spirit), the lamb, four living creatures, twenty-four elders and innumerable angels and heavenly hosts?

If the word, "come up here"-Rev. 4:1 means the lift-up to heaven of the saints isn't it natural all the saints should participate in the service? After the rapture the saints should be the one with the Lord and worship Him with joy, but where are they in the service? If the Chapter 4:1 means the rapture why the saints were not allowed to join the services?

However, we find the saints in chapter 7:9-17 and why? The fact must be that the rapture was not done by the time of service before the throne in chapter 4 and so, it seems proper that 'come up here' means an individual invitation for apostle John.

The Definition of a New Song

Twenty-four elders were singing a new song. We can imagine ourselves singing this new song to praise the Lord when we come up to heaven. If we do not know this new song we might be unable to sing together before the glorious throne.

This new song is a praise of our new spiritual experience. When we experience the born-again we sing our endless thankfulness to the Lord. Moreover, when we are filled with the Holy Spirit, we can give thanks and praise at higher level than before. As our faith grows and our relationship with the Lord gets closer we experience our praise comes from our deeper and higher love for the Lord.

Our faith is like climbing a high mountain. As we come up the mountain higher and higher we marvel at new wonderful beauty of view. So, the level of our faith gets deeper and higher, we come to be filled with new joy and praise. This is how to exercise a new song at the church on earth. We take up our cross, walk through the narrow road for the Kingdom of Heaven, and at last we see the Lord and fall down before the God's throne. Can you imagine the joy and glory? With this new experience, a new song will burst out.

> Jesus, the very thought of thee.
> With sweetness fills my breast ;
> but sweeter far thy face to see.
> And in thy presence rest.

Yosemite National Park in California is renowned to be one of the most beautiful and magnificent parks in the US and Koreans gave it a nickname of "Mt. Keumkang in America." There is little rain from April to October in southern California, so this half-desert area has no thick forest and most hills are covered with dried grass.

However, even the hottest summer time of July and August when one enters the hill road to Yosemite National Park one can find a dense forest with fresh air. As one drives up higher, there are gorgeous view with pine trees and clear stream in the valley. Three-hour drive takes one to the Yosemite Valley with falls and cliffs like screens on its both sides. The Yosemite Fall offers 4 km-long splendor most tourists leave the park because they think this point has the most beautiful view.

However, about one and half-hour more drive leads to the peak of glacier point, which provides with the complete view of snow-covered mountain tops at Yosemite. These high peaks are covered with snow even in summer, and its valleys' stream turns into falls.

This is truly spectacular. Its highest peak requires about five hours more drive and it is cold enough to wear sweaters in summer and there are full blossoms of flowers like spring. Many people flock into Yosemite from all over the world, and they should book a hotel room at least several months earlier some tourists sing their folk songs when they get excited and moved by the spectacular view.

When we see the face of our Lord how can we sing an old hymn? The joy of the day will be directly proportional to the weight of our cross in delivering God's message on earth with pain and sweat. "I consider that our present sufferings are not worth comparing with the glory that will be revealed in us" (Roman 8:18). It must be our confession when we obey to the Lord's word in spite of various sufferings. We take up our cross to follow Jesus, give thanks in all circumstances, and practice a new song always. Someday the saints who were faithful servants can sing a new song more joyfully in the Kingdom of God. "Every nation, tribe, people and language"(rev. 7:9) will participate in the Kingdom of God in the future.

God does not have deep concern with United States of America or Korea. His primary concern is with the Kingdom of God that will be accomplished in the last days. If he blessed and concerned a nation, he does it when it is required to accomplish the Kingdom of God. God's providence is focused to the history of the church. The church is the core of history and the seedbed of the Kingdom of God. We realize the great importance of church existence today and its missions as they were to the Israel in the Old Testament era.

This book emphasizes what church as a focus of history has to do his mission when the prophesied signs appear at the end. We have to invest all we have in order to accomplish our missions just as a merchant of pearl in his parable. Many historians believe that the rise and fall of a nation depends on the powerful forces, but that was not the reason for the fall of Babylon and Russia. The communist nations collapsed even though whole nation had been armed with the ideology for which brain washed from kindergarten insisting that the ideology control the rise and fall of a nation.

The historian, Dr. Paul Kennedy, insists that the rise and fall of a nation depends on the national economic power. Of course there is some truth in that but Sodom and Gomorrah were not ruined because of weak economy. The reason of their fall was because they sinned morally, staying away from God, and the rise and fall of a nation after all is considered to be in the hand of God. The history had started by him who is a creator and the end of the history will be done also by him who is the final judge. The past, present, and future are in the hand of God. God placed him far above all rule, authority, power, dominion and things under his feet after the Lord had loyally accomplished the mission of the redemption, becoming sacrifice himself on the cross(eph. 1:21-22). The Lord is a controller of the history. All international events of history seem to be managed by presidents or premiers of super powers, but we will firmly realize while reading this book that God controls it with invisible hand in the back. Because Revelation clearly shows us that the history is under way as it has been prophesied by him.

Chapter 6
The Lamb Opening the Seven Seals

What Was the Sealed Scroll?

When Revelation was written, it was the time that the papers like we use today was not invented yet. The scroll that time was made out of thinned lamb's skin and wrote on it using brush with ink. It was called scroll because that was made out of long piece of lamb's skin. Therefore, we find the word, 'scroll' a lot in the Bible.

"He asked me, what do you see? I answered, I see a flying scroll"(Zech. 5:2).

"It is written about me in the scroll"(Psalm 40:7).

"A scroll was found in the citadel of Ecbatana in the province of Media"(Ezra 6:2).

The seven sealed scrolls were made out of seven pieces of lamb's skin that were tied up together by twine through the drilled holes which means a book of seven pages in modern expression.

What is Meant by Sealing Seven Seals?

Sealing means secrecy

In ancient time of our country a king sent the confidential instruction to a local official directly through a royal messenger after sealing the letter that was written in ink with writing brush on the window paper. Nobody could open the sealed royal letter on the way.

Being sealed by seven seals means seven secrets

The sealed seven pages of the book that will be accomplished by God in history. Essentially, man does not know about tomorrow but the beginning, ongoing and end of history is all controlled by the hand of God. He is absolutely a controller of history.

A builder of a house makes a blue-print first and build it according to the plan

When someone try to build any building, makes a blue-print for the building. Moreover, wouldn't God have the blue-print of history when he is going to build a new heaven and a new earth? We can believe history is ruled over according to his blue-print.

All the prophecies that had been prophesied through the prophets in the Old Testament era have been accomplished and in the New Testament era today's history is under way according to the prophecy of Jesus.

While I was studying Revelation I became sure to understand

that the seven seals represent the seven secrets of the seven historical events that will be accomplished by God at the last days.

The Time of Sealing

The sealed scroll had already been revealed to Daniel. When we study chapter 12 of Daniel in detail:

> "But you, Daniel, close up and seal the words of the scroll until the time of the end, many will go here and there to increase knowledge"(12:4).

Daniel wanted to know the contents of the scroll and asked him again:

> "My Lord, what will the outcome of all this be?"(Daniel 12:8).

He replied:

> "Go your way, Daniel, because the words are closed up and sealed until the time of the end. Many will be purified, made spotless and refined, but the wicked will continue to be wicked. none of the wicked will understand, but those who are wise will understand" (Daniel 12:9-10).

But let's refer to the following Scriptures:

"For he chose us in him before the creation of the world"(Eph.1:4)
"From one man he made every nation of men, that they should inhabit the whole earth ; and he determined the times set for them and the exact places where they should live"(act, 17:26).

Above Scriptures tell us that God chose us before creation and set the times of all nations. that is, it shows that the words of the scroll until "the time of the end" means that it will be opened in the last days and then gave to Daniel a hint to know it as follows:

"Many will go here and there to increase knowledge"(Daniel 12:4).

In Hebrew, go here and there is "Eshiteru." In the Old Testament, used this word several times:

"Run to and for through the streets of Jerusalem look around and take note"(Jer 5:1).
"They shall run and fro seeking the word of the Lord"(Am 8:12).
"Those seven are the eyes of the Lord, which range through the whole earth"(Zech 4:10).

When I study the word which I quote "Eshiteru" means "fast traffic." "Running come and go" and "fast move as eye ball."
Now you could reach the conclusion that human will invent the fast traffic machines in the last days. That is the sign of the last days then Jesus will open the seals.

Let us study when human began to invent the fast traffic machines in the history of the world. We have to remember that there was not any fast traffic machine when Revelation was written. It may be the fastest traffic way to ride a horse.

But Thomas Newcoman in England, invented the steam engine in 1712, so the train and steam ship were invented that human could take trip very fast. Around 1770s, the gasoline engine was invented that the automobile began to run, airplane began to fly, we made the earth as one days traffic era.

We, therefore, could realize the hint in Daniel 12:4, "Eshiteru." It prophesied the fast traffic at the end of history by the development of the transportation. The fastest transportation during the time of Daniel was horsemen or chariots running by horses. But man revolutionized the transportation since 1700 A.D. By the development of ships, steam-engines, automobiles, airplanes and missile. Especially the development of science in this century has been remarkably accelerated. Therefore, the prophecy of "many will go here and there" seems appropriate to regards it as a symbolic prophecy that started to open the seals after 1700s A.D. The reason why it had started from the 1700 A.D. will be explained again in detail at next chapter.

Now we could reach for the conclusion that after 1770s Jesus would open the seal.

The Purpose of Opening the Seals

When we study 1 Thessalonians 5:1-11, it says,

"For you know very well that the day of the Lord will come like a thief in the night"(5:2).

But it also says,

"You, brothers, are not in the darkness so that this day should surprise you like a thief"(5:4).

Why would not the day come like a thief to the Christians? It is because the Lord had already prophesied the events as the signs of the second coming and also we can see what Jesus is accomplishing the prophesied events opening the seals by Himself one by one in the history. Of course, this is not to say that we know the day of his coming. It is not Biblical to know the date because the date is unknown to any person but only God. We can awake ourselves thinking his coming is near when we see the accomplishment of his prophecies. Our Lord said that ;

"When you see these things happening, you know that the Kingdom of God is near"(Luke 21:21).

It is appropriate to think that eschatological prophecies of Jesus and Revelation's prophecies are historical clock that inform us time of the Second Advent. We should wake ourselves up and finish our task, Great Commission mission in the given time with understanding and watching at the time that is shown to us by our Lord.

The events of opening the seven seals were given to us as a valuable prophecies like a clock that tells us God's time, but we have made the historical clock given by God useless by imputing to the events that will happen after the rapture. The events after chapter 6:1 is not the things that will happen after the rapture, but before the rapture.

We would watch the fulfillment of the prophecies of the seven seals very carefully because that are the signs of his Second Advent. Jesus repeated for emphasizing that the followings ;

"Now when these things begin to take place, stand up and raise your heads, because your redemption is drawing near" (Luke 21:28).

"When these things take place, you know that the Kingdom of God is near"(Luke 21:31).

"When you see all these things, you know that he is near, at the very gates, truly away until all these things have taken away, but my word will not pass away"(Matthew 24:33-35).

The purpose of the opening the seven seals is to wake us up to finish our task, carry out the great commission at the last days.

Six Premises of the Interpretation
on the Seven Seals

In order to interpret the above Scriptures correctly the events that accomplish the prophecies should contain the following elements:

The events must be the one that happen really in history
I have studied Revelation. As I described in chapter 6, the

prophecies of Revelation would be accomplished in the history of the world of last days. Even some scholars may not agree with me.

The events must be the great world events

Jesus is the universal, the Gospel is also universal, so Second Coming of Jesus would be universal. If some event happened at a small city in a country, then how all of the world wide Christians could know the event as a signs of his Coming? The event may be started at a small city but have to be known by mass media all over the would. So that all of the Christians in the world know the event to be waken up.

The events must be the one that happen in the last days

As I already described in this chapter on the time to open the seals it must be happen after 1700 A.D., which is the last days era. Because all of those prophecies in the seven seals are the signs of the Second Coming of Jesus.

The events must be in accord with the eschatological prophecies of Jesus in the 4 Gospels

In Matthew chapter 24, Mark 13, and Luke 21 there are many prophecies of Jesus which are the signs of the second coming. Same person, Jesus, gave Revelation to John that would be accord with the prophecy of Jesus in the Gospel. I can not even imagine to have any conflict between the prophecy in Gospel and the prophecy in Revelation.

***The events must be in accord with other eschatological
prophecies in the Bible***

As we believe the Bible as the word of God which were inspired
by the Holy Spirit for the writing it. In the Letters of the New
Testament there are some verses regarding the signs of Jesus
coming back to us. When we interpret them, have to be accord
with Revelation because same Holy Spirit inspired.

***The events should not be interpreted intolerantly in favor of
certain denominations or individuals***

Mr. Tae Sun Park, who is one of the Korean heresy leader said
"I am the Olive Tree in Revelation 1:3" and no one could be
saved without by me who is the Olive Tree in the last day. He
finally was dismissed by the Korean Presbyterian Church. The
Igrecia denomination in Philippines also insist them as the Angel
in Revelation 7:2-3. I can not accept this kind of interpretations.

I have studied Revelation on the above six premises and wrote
in this book.

Chapter 7
Opening the First Seal
(Western Colonial War)

"I watched as the lamb opened the first of the seven seals. Then I heard one of the four living creatures say in a voice like thunder, come! I looked, and there before me was a white horse! Its rider held a bow, and he was given a crown, and he rode out as a conqueror bent on conquest"(Rev. 6:1-2).

Interpretation of the Text

In this text there are important vocabularies:white horse, rider, crown, bow, conquest so on. Let us study those words.

White Horse

Horse:The horse in the first century, when Revelation was written, was the most important animal in the war. The chariot and horsemen were a very powerful army unit same as today's tank or armored unit. So it is appropriate that four horses in Chapter

6:1-8 are regarded as representing some wars. Therefore, the white horse, the red horse, the black horse and the pale horse are in those verses to be regarded as four world wide wars that will be broken out at in the last days in the history of the world. It is the providence of God to let Christians wake up from a sleep and fulfil the eschatological missions as the four wars break out.

Crown

Crown is the symbol of a king and so the rider was a king of a nation. But we do not know which nation's king is. A king use to be the supreme commander, riding a white horse and commanded the war at that time.

Bow and arrow

A bow and arrow are not the weapon that are capable to do mass killing at once like various modern weapons that is a weapon to shoot people down one by one. Above interpretations indicate that a king with great power and technique would bring a victory in the war by shooting people one by one with bow and arrow. The bow he has the bow of Gospel. Why the Gospel was revealed as the bow and arrow? Arrow shoot down people one by one. The Gospel also shoot at a person's soul with the arrow of word of God to repent. Children of any Christian family would not naturally become Christian but when they receive Jesus in their heart as the King and Savior. Any husbands would not automatically have faith when his wife has faith. Even a Christian nation was declared but whole people of a nation would not become Christian when a nation declared herself a Christian country. Revelation by the arrow seems to be very rational because the arrows of the Gospel that were shot at individuals one by one make him repent and become Christian by receiving Jesus as the Savior and the King.

The rider

Who would be the rider on the white horse? The interpretations about the white horse by scholars are various as follows:

1. The Gospel itself
2. The antichrist.
3. A king of certain nation.
4. The Christ.

The above show variety in interpretations about the white horse. There are wide range of interpretations from Roman conqueror to Christ and moreover are extremely contrasting one of Christ and antichrist from the above interpretations.

I choose number 4, that the crown represents a king. But number 1, 2 are not a king. Number 3 is about king, but it is not the events that happened at the last days and also not a worldwide event.

But the one appears in the Rev. 19:11-16, rides a white horse with name written as "King of kings and the Lord of lords"(19:16). Jesus is indeed the universal savior and the King of kings.

The first seal is very important. When first interpretation were wrong the next chronology would be all wrong accordingly because historical events are all in chronological order. It is the same reason that all buttons of a shirt would be fastened wrong when the first one buttoned up wrong. That's why God revealed the interpretation of the rider in the white horse in Rev. 19:11-16.

Conquest

The rider seem to be very much powerful and wise for conquest in this war. Jesus was the rider and his conquest means the extension of his kingdom, the Kingdom of God, which is the Christian church.

This prophecy is that the Christian church will be expanded to all over the world in the last days as one of the signs of Second Advent of Jesus. There is same prophecy of Jesus in Matthew 24:14.

"And this good news of the Kingdom will be proclaimed throughout the world, as a testimony to all the nations ; and then the end will come"

The Word of Jesus is almighty which created the universe by his word(John 1:1-3). When Jesus said a word, for example, "Nazarus, come out!" and the dead man came out of the grave, when Jesus rebuked the winds and the sea and there was dead calm. He said the Gospel will spread out to all over the world and this mighty word must be fulfilled some day in the history of the world.

White horse

Christianity was the white people's religion until 1800 A.D., even it is worldwide religion now. The strong missionary movement arose from British churches by 1800 A.D. Since then the Gospel began to spread out very quickly to all over the world by the western missionaries through the waves of the western colonialism. The white horse, therefore, the western colonial war.

Fulfillment of This Prophecy

The Great Commission of Jesus(until 1800 A.D.)

Jesus commandeers to His Disciples ;

"Go into all the world and proclaim the good news"(Mark 16:15).

"Go therefore and make disciples of all nations, baptizing them in the name of the Father and of the Son and of the Holy Spirit, and teaching them to obey everything that I have commanded you. And remember, I am with you always, to the end of the age" (Matt. 28:19-20).

It is the reason to exist the Christians and his church in this earth to carry out the Great Commission as the first priority. But the Jerusalem Church in Acts did not realize it, and concentrated only for the Jerusalem Church growth. She grew. Male believers reached 5,000 members(Acts 4:4). They did not send even one missionary to Judea or Samaria but care about only Jerusalem church. God, therefore, allowed a persecution on the Jerusalem Church and even Deacon Stephen was killed by them. Because of the severe persecution began against the Jerusalem Church and all except the apostles were scattered throughout the countryside of Judea, and Samaria, the Christian mission was started by St. Paul and Barnabas from early church in Acts. The Apostle Paul tried to spread the Gospel to whole world, sacrificing his life but had reached only to the Asia Minor and a part of Europe.

The St. Thomas Church still exists in southern part of India and they think that the disciple Thomas came to India and sowed the seed of the Gospel there in 1st Century but no any historical or archeological evidence to prove it.

There is a monument in China to prove a Catholic missionary spread the Gospel there in 7th century but we don't know any Christian Churches existed in China at that time. An article recently discovered in Japan that Christian church was in Japan in 8th century before Buddhism came in to Japan.

When Jinghis Khan invited the Catholic priests into China after conquering the Europe and Christian church was in China for a while but it could not exist continually. A Korean Church historian, Rev. Yang Sun Kim, made an interesting statement of his study that a rock in the shape of the cross found in a Buddhist temple in the northern province of Pyongan Book Do indicates an evidence that the Christianity already existed in Korea around 12th Century but there are no archeological evidence to support his statement.

Christianity was tried to become a worldwide religion but it remained only as an European religion until 17th Century and could not be a worldwide religion like today. But the Spain and Portugal who were Catholic nations in the 16th Century started a colonial movement that made Catholicism began to spread rapidly into the world. They made the enemy struck with fear first by bombardment from warships before landing to colonize her and then started to spread the Gospel.

The Great Commission of Jesus from 1800 A.D.

The missionary movement of the Protestant Church was insignificant until the beginning of 1800 A.D. There were only six missionary councils and about two hundred missionaries in the whole world until 1784. The missionary movement of the Protestant Church had started first by the Moravian Brothers Denomination of Germany. The Moravian brought an awakening in the evangelical movement of the Christianity by the ardent passion of sending out missionaries in ratio of one to every 67 persons within only twenty year period from 1732 to 1752.

England became the Super Power in 19th Century

England became the super power to have the large territory of the colonies in Africa, North and South America, and Asia. English navy and navy ships were all over the world for protecting English immigrants and her territories of the colonies and English merchant ships were almost everywhere in the world. The missionary movement from England was possible and succeeded because of her protection and the transportations.

John Wesley

The full scale missionary movement of Protestant Church had started from England in 1800s. John Wesley who was influenced by the Moravian began the revival and awakening movement in the entire England with a well-known slogan of "The world is my parish." A motivation of missionary arises from passion of saving a soul. But the motivation does not arise without the revival of the Holy Spirit challenged to many young people for dedicating their life as the missionaries who became great missionary man power later.

William Carey

The great missionary movement was started by William Carey (1761-1834) who was born in a poor family in England. He was very wise and smart from the child age, specially had a talent for foreign language, so he studied Hebrew, Latin, French, and Dutch. When he was 18 years old he was ordained as a Baptist minister.

One day he read a book "World Journey" by Cook, inspired to start missionary movement because there are many tribes who do not know Jesus and worship idols even killing their children for sacrificing to their gods. He thought that we Christians have to obey the Great Commission for the lost souls in the British colonies and other part of the world.

When the Baptist pastors meeting was held William Carey stood up and suggested to the missionaries to foreign nations for saving these lost souls but the chairman rejected his proposal. He was so disappointed and wrote and published a book, "An Enquiry into the Obligation of Christians to use Means for the Conversion of the Heathens." Many Christians read that book and inspired for the Great Commission. And they were so much challenged and joined with him for sending missionaries.

In 1792, William Carey with 12 pastors organized "The British Baptist Missionary Society" which became the first mission organization in England. He was supported by the missionary society members, went to India as a missionary and served faithfully his whole life until God called him to heaven.

It was beginning for the great missionary movement from England. Many mission societies began to organized:interdenominational, London Missionary Society in 1795, Netherland Missionary Society in 1797, Church Missionary Society in 1799, The British Bible Society in 1804. So on. Since then the Gospel have been spreading out to over the world. From 1800 A.D. to 1900, for one century the Gospel have reached 82 nations, but from 1900 to the present only 13 nations.

The Table of the Missionary Outreach

1737:South Africa

1776:Indonesia

1788:Malaysia

1793:India

1795:Sierra Leone

1797:Society Islands

1805:South West Africa

1807:China

1811:Iran

1812:Ceylon, Burma

1815:Egypt

1816:Haiti

1817:Botswana

1818:Malacca

1820:Iraq, Israel, Argentina, Peru, Ecuador

1821:Chile

1822:Celebes

1823:Lebanon, Fiji Island

1824:Syria

1825:Bolivia

1826:Mexico

1828:Thailand, Gina

1829:Tunisia

1830:Turkey, Liberia, Samoa

1833:Venezuela

1835:Borneo

1841:Cameron

1842:Nigeria, Gabon

1844:Kenya, Ethiopia

1847:Togaland

1848:Jordan

1849:Pakistan, Nicaragua Castalia

1850:Solomon Island

1852:Canary Islands

1855:Brazil

1858:Sumatra

1859:Rhodesia

1860:Tanganyika

1862:Senegal

1865:Taiwan

1870:New Guinea, Dahomey

1875:Morocco, Somalia

1876:Uganda

1878:Angola, Congo, Belgium

1880:Mozambican

1881:Algeria, Cuba, Guatemala

1884:Korea

1885:Arabia

1888:Libya, Paraguay

1889:Dominica
1895:Japan
1896:Honduras
1898:Bolivia, El Salvador, Panama
1899:Philippine, Sudan

1902:Laos
1903:Mindanao
1911:Vietnam
1913:Ivory Cost
1915:Cambodia
1916:Guinea
1920:Central Africa
1921:Bolt
1924:Niger
1925:Chad
1926:Burundi
1950:Nepal
1955:Tibet

Chapter 8
Opening the Second Seal
(War of Ideologies)

"When the Lamb opened the second seal, I heard the second living creature say, 'Come!' Then another horse came out, a fiery red one. Its rider was given power to take peace from the earth and to make men slay each other. To him was given a large sword"(Rev. 6:3-4).

Interpretation of the Text

The second horse is red. The rider of the red horse has a large sword to destroy peace on earth. He destroys the world's peace, leading us to kill each other. As I mentioned previously the "horse" signifies war or battle. "Red", this bloody color stands for wars or revolution. "A large sword" means military power or political power which is the control behind the military. "To take peace from the earth" infers that the world peace would be threatened because of this red power. "To make men slay each other" is one of the characteristics of the red power. They deceive people, this deception causes them to kill each other in order to destroy peace on earth.

The Christian mission movement which started in England in the early eighteenth century influenced by western imperialism can be interpreted as the appearance of the white horse. The next, the red horse infers that something big would happen after eighteenth century. The rider of the red horse would have a great military and political power, for he has a large sword. This red power threatens the world causing nations and races to fight and kill each other.

Then, what was the biggest event in history of threatening the world peace after the eighteenth century?

Power of Killing Each Other

To answer this question, let us look at those people who took peace from the earth after the 1800's.

First, there was Napoleon Bonaparte I(1769-1821) in France. He was inaugurated as the first Director in February 1799. In 1804 he became an emperor through a national vote. From his first rule as a Director until 1814 he had covered the European countries with blood, victorious conquer though in 60 battles. Though he led French armies in campaigns he did not cause the French people kill each other to expand their power. It is not proper to label him as "causing people to kill each other."

Next, Adolf Hitler(1889-1945). He was born in northern Austria and became the head of Nazi Party in 1912. He started the Second World War and threatened the world with fear killing six million Jews and other people. He also led the German army wherever he went but he did not have the people kill each other. Neither did Mussolini of Italy nor Dorzo of Japan, divided their own people and caused them to kill each other to in order to expand their powers, though they all threatened the world.

Who is it, then? It must be Nikolai Lenin(1870-1924) of Russia who started the Communist Revolution. He studied law at Kazan University, learning Communism from Karl Marx, and initiated the Communist Revolution in 1917. In 1918 he summoned a Constitutional Congress and established the Soviet Union. Through his bloody revolution the first communist government in history was established. After that the communist movement was like epidemic, resulting in a half of the world population living under communist governments for about 70 years whether they wanted or not ; Eastern Europe, China with one-fourth the world population, Vietnam, North Korea, Cuba, Angola, etc. Communism continues to shed blood in many places throughout the world.

The expansion of communism was done not by Russian military force but by proletarian ideology which brought success. Russian proletariats armed with communist ideology arose revolution in its own country to kill each other and expanded its power.

Dialectical Historical Advancement
of Communism

The strategy of killing each other comes from dialectical philosophy. Dialectics originated from Hegel, a German philosopher, and his philosophy states that history develops the principles of thesis, antithesis, and synthesis. In other words, if one principle comes in called thesis, then the opposite principle called antithesis takes place. These two principles compete each other and finally they are integrated into another principle called synthesis. This synthesis is taken place a new thesis competing with a new antithesis and again integrated together creating a new synthesis. Dialectic insists that history develops likewise.

Lenin, however, changed one word from Hegel's dialectical development ; he used "struggle" instead of "competition." He saw that historical development was done not by competing but by struggling that one power struggles with another. When one destroys the other history develops. He believed that the Russian Revolution would not be successful without this method. Lenin saw those extorters as "thesis" ; the emperor and his followers of the Czarist Russia, usurers, landowners, and Orthodox Church leaders who were under the power of extorters. He regarded the proletarians, farmers and laborers, the main group of the Bolshevik revolution as "antithesis." Because of his belief on historical development by struggles he insisted that they would fight against the oppressors taking their possession and would kill them. By modeling this dialectical theory of historical development communism was spread all over the world.

Therefore, wherever communism was imported they killed each other. Hundreds of thousands of Chinese were killed likewise and it did the same thing during the Korean War. Wherever communism went Vietnam, Cuba, Angola or elsewhere many people were killed under dialectical strategy. That is the theory and practice of communists' régime dealing with the world of communism. Thus, it is quite appropriate to interpret the appearance of the red horse as the cruel war of communist ideology.

Because it's theory is based on a materialistic view of history communism fell into atheism, no judgment of God, and merciless struggles. Denying God they do not admit the privilege of freedom that God has given to all human beings such as freedom of speech, association, meeting, and of faith. They have shed Christian blood mostly in history and treating human lives as animals or machines.

God's Purpose for Allowing Communism

It is written in the text, "Its rider was given power···"(v. 4). Who and why gave communism power?

Romans 13:1 says, "···for there is no authority except that which God has established." There is a serious question. Why did God give the communists power through which persecuted Christianity so harshly, imprisoning and killing saints, closing churches. The answer might be to fulfill the prophecy of the signs of the Second

Coming of the Lord. As the white horse appeared to fulfill the prophecy in Matthew 24:14, so did the red horse to fulfill the prophecy written in Luke 21:29-31 ;

"He told them this parable:look at the fig tree and all the trees. When they sprout leaves, you can see for yourselves and know that summer is near. Even so, when you see these things happening, you know that the kingdom of God is near."

The Lord prophesied when the day of his Second Coming is near the fig tree and all the trees would sprout leaves. The fig tree is a symbol of Israel. It is a prophecy that the Israelite would become independent as a new country before the world just as new leaves are sprouting out in the spring after a winter's sleep. When the biblical scholars insisted that the prophecy of Israel's independence would be fulfilled one day historians viewed it impossible because a small and weak country under over 400 colonial controls would be identified with a ruling power. This prophecy, however, came true:Israel declared its independence on May 14, 1948 after 2000 years' sojourning, scattered all over the world under various persecutions. They had desires of freedom and independence. In September 1949 Israel joined the United Nations ; it was after 2000 years after Jesus had told the prophecy.

Jesus said that all the trees sprout leaves, too. In other words, all the small nations in the world would be independent like Israel. All the small and weak countries and various ethnic groups under powers of imperialism would gain their independence just about the time when Israel did.

Breaking Up the Imperialism

It is common sense that a winner of a war expands its territory. World War II, however, was different ; it is hard to explain with common sense. All the winning countries had lost their territory. First, look at the USA. Her territory has been reduced because Cuba and the Philippines, which used to be her colonies have been now become independent. France is the same ; her Asian countries including Vietnam, Laos, Cambodia, and Northern Africa such as Libya and Algeria which produce oil are now independent from her. Then Great Britain was even worse. There once was a saying that they had no sunset in Great Britain, for her power was expanded to Canada, Australia, India, and Africa. Her colonies reach around the world. However, they have become independent and became a poor country from super power. Therefore, the World War II became hard to understand.

It was a blessing of God that the western world had received the Gospel first and become prosperous and strong. God used them for evangelizing the world. They, however, had exploited the poor and the weak with their power and wealth from God, which is against God's justice and righteousness. It is, therefore, God's justice to set the poor and the oppressed free from the oppression and control of other powers.

How has God accomplished this in human history? First, God worked through President Wilson(Woodrow Wilson, 1856-1924). In January 1918, after the World War I, Wilson declared a

14-diplomatic policy to reconstruct permanent world peace. The key words included breaking up a secret diplomacy, free flight in public sea, breaking down an economic wall among nations, building an international office for maintaining peace, reduction of armaments, and respect of the self-determination of peoples. When the self-determination of peoples was issued, small and weak nations in the world like Korea started becoming independent.

On August 10, 1941, during the World War II the Atlantic Charter was issued by President Franklin D. Roosevelt (1882-1945) and the Prime Minister of Great Britain, Winston Churchill(1874-1965). After a four-day meeting on the Prince of Wales while she was anchored at an Argentinan port in New Portland the principle of self-determination of peoples was included in this Charter, too.

It was not completed yet, however, with these declarations and the Charter to accomplish independence of weak and small nations. The western colonial powers would not allow them to be independent. After the Atlantic Charter Churchill insisted that it would not apply to Great Britain's colonies such as India.

After the World War II, Vietnam established and declared a democratic republic, but France started the Indochina War in 1946 to control Vietnam with military force. This effort, however, was not successful because of increasing national consciousness in Vietnam. The Netherlands also attacked Indonesia twice(June 1947 and December 1948) after Indonesia established a republic. Confronting critiques from the world and national consciousness, the Netherlands admitted Indonesia's independence.

In 1951, Iran tried to nationalize the Anglo Oil Company, which belonged to Great Britain. So Great Britain protected it with its Air Force and Marines. In 1956 Nasser was trying to nationalize the Suez Canal. France, Great Britain, and Israel had a war to keep this canal. This attempt try was also not successful.

What was the primary reason? Some said that it was because of economical poverty and the military weakness of the colonial countries after the World War Ⅱ. It was not persuaded. It was more than possible for the Great Britain, France, and Israel to attack Egypt, which had little armament in 1956. Whenever these kinds of incidents happened, the USA influenced them not to use military forces, for using military forces might cause the USSR to attack somewhere and that might lead to the World War Ⅲ. In fact, on the same day when the three countries attacked Egypt (october 24, 1956) did not the USSR attack Budapest, Hungary with tanks and mass murder the young Hungarians who claimed freedom?

After the end of the World War Ⅱ, the world was divided into two:communist and the democratic realm, and they entered the era of the Cold War. They had confronted each other with nuclear weapons that have power to destroy tens of the thousands of the earth carrying missiles. If they would start a nuclear war, it was certain that there would not be a winner or a loser for it would destroy the world. If the Great Britain moved her main force units to India when India attempted to be independent, then her independence would not be possible. God allowed the communists to have temporal power and put the European main force in Europe. In the mean time, he let the strong rule over the weak, which was against God's justice. The reason for that was to fulfill the prophecy of the last day written in Luke 21:29-31 and to awake Christians all over the world. In the past 100 years, we have not had at least 10 countries had achieve independence. After the World War II, however, we have seen about 100 countries obtaining their independences for about 40 years. I believe this was a miracle in human history.

The age of the white horse can be interpreted as the colonial period. The purpose of all the battles of that period(even World War II) was to expand territories and to grab power. During the colonial period, the Western European powers controlled over most of the world. North and South Americas and most of then African countries belonged to Western Europe. In Asia only Japan, China, and Thailand were independent and other countries were ruled by either Japan or western European countries. The powers oppressed the weak nations under colonialism, despising God-given human dignity and freedom. They exploited in their colonies segregating races and torturing, imprisoning, and killing the leaders who wanted to be independent from them. The oppressed were not strong enough to resist them, but appealed to God for their agonies. My grandfather was imprisoned while he was work in an independent movement under Japanese colonialism, resulting in my family's bankruptcy and I was forced under the circumstances to give up even middle school, following my elementary years.

Most western European countries are Christian ones or influenced by Christianity. In spite of that Colonialism and colonial wars were against Biblical principles because they oppressed and exploited the weak. Was it coincidence when communism arose and declared Christianity as opium? I think that it was an inevitable result from God's justice and righteousness in human history. Some regard communism as illegitimate child of Christianity, which seems right and we have to repent deeply. If we oppress the weak with power God would judge us with his power. If the USA still behaves as the super power controlling the weak with economic and military power then God will judge her through historical judgment before long. We should put our knowledge into practice that justice is a power. I have seen numerous cases of discrimination over the past 30 years since my immigration, and I have been hurt when I meet those who discriminate inside the church. I want to ask a question:"What is the reason for the church? If the church is ignorant concerning social justice or are they joining with social injustice?" The age of the white horse ended up when the age of the red horse came just as the Lord prophesied. Colonialism would never come again in the world history.

That was God's first wake up call. How many Christians were martyred because of the red horse? Those Christian countries that received the Gospel first became blind to colonialism and were not aware of the red horse coming. Why did God allow the red horse to persecute the Christianity? The Church had not been salt to the corrupted secular world and she, the church would not care for them. She was corrupted with them. She became a servant of politics, falling in love with nationalism, but did not take the responsibility of prophetic roles in order to convey God's Word. Thus, God allowed communism to stay for a while so that the church would be awakened.

For a reference, I provide a list of countries that obtained their independence during the era of secession of the Cold War, beginning in 1945 and the years when they joined the United Nations. It is called a history of miracle.

1945:USSR(1945-1991)

1946:Afghanistan, Iceland, Sweden, and Thailand

1947:Pakistan

1948:Myanmar

1949:Israel

1950:Indonesia

1953:Romania

1955:Albania, Austria, Bulgaria, Cambodia, Finland, Hungary, Ireland, Italy, Jordan, Laos, Libya, Nepal, Portugal, and Spain

1956:Morocco, Sudan, Tunisia, Sri Lanka

1957:Ghana, Malaysia

1958:Guiana

1960:Benin, Burkina Faso, Cameroon, Cyprus, Gabon, Madagascar, Mali, Niger, Nigeria, Senegal, Somalia,

Togo, Zaire

1961:Mauritania, Mongolia, Sierra Leone

1962:Algeria, Burundi, Jamaica, Rwanda, Trinidad & Tobago, Uganda

1963:Kenya, Kuwait

1964:Malawi, Malta, Zambia

1965:Gambia, Maldives, Singapore

1966:Barbados, Botswana, Lesotho

1968:Equatorial, Mauritius, Swaziland

1970:Fiji

1971:Bahrain, Oman, Qatar, and United Arab Emirates

1973:Bahamas

1974:Bangladesh, Grenada, Guinea-Bissau, and Guyana

1975:Comoros, Mozambique, Papua New Guinea, and Sao Tome E Principe, Suriname

1976:Angola, Seychelles, and Western Samoa

1977:Djibouti, Vietnam

1978:Solomon Ireland

1979:Dominica, St. Lucia

1980:St. Vincent & The Grenadines, Zimbabwe

1981:Antigua & Barbuda, Belize, Vanuatu

1983:St. Kitts & Nevis

1984:Brunei

Chapter 9
Opening the Third Seal
(Economic Warfare)

"When the lamb opened the third seal, I heard the living creature say 'Come!' I looked, and there before me was a pair of black horses! Its rider was holding a pair of scales in his hand. Then I heard what sounded like a voice among the four living creatures, saying, "A quart of wheat for a day's wages, and three quarts of barley for a day's wages, and do not damage the oil and the wine!"(Rev 5:5-6, NIV)

Textual Analysis

The black horses designate the coming of another war after the ending of the ideological war.

"Its rider was holding a pair of scales in his hand."

A scale has been inherited from the ancient times in order to weigh the merchandise. Therefore, a scale signifies trade and commerce. It is a prophecy stating that after the war of ideology, the era of worldwide economic warfare is coming.

"A day's wage, one Denarius" is a monetary unit of Israel. It equals a wage for one day's labor working. They pay about $70 a day in the USA today. It is probably similar to that amount of money.

"Wine" stands for a thankful and rejoicing heart, and "olive oil" means powerful life by the Holy Spirit.

A Prophecy of the Economic Warfare

The third horse is a black one and a "horse" that signifies a war the rider has a scale in his hands. And in verse 6 it was shown to John that barley and wheat were measured and sold. Today we see scales in many commercial stores.

A scale manifests commerce and a horse signifies a war. Therefore, it is a prophecy of an upcoming economic war.

As the white horse represents western colonialism was defeated by the red horse which represents communist revolution, the war of ideology would be defeated by the black horse symbolizing an economic war.

In the early 1970s it seemed that the communists' régime was victoriously expanding into the world. So people were concerned about the world domination of communism.

I have stated from the early 60s in my expository sermons communism would end and a worldwide economic war would then follow. At that time, however, you were not able to find even the word, "economic war" in the newspapers. But now, this is reported everyday. Economic wars are true factors in the world. So, therefore, the economic war has already begun.

Economic Warfare

Looking at world history, there have been conflicts or battles between regions or nations, as well as international economic warfare. Unlike the previous battles among regions, the two world wars in the 20th century were historical events.

The time is now for the world economic war. All of the issues have been centered to the expanding of economic affairs. Presidents of the nations visit other countries for the purpose of expanding trade, economic cooperation, technical support, or the economic advancement of their countries, not for political or diplomatic issues.

Until the early 1960s a diplomats dealt with only diplomatic affairs, but from the 1970s they would now take care of marketing, reporting the investigations, and even selling products of their country.

For example, the Korean government has recently joined the Foreign Affairs and the Department of Commerce together and established the Department of Foreign-Commercial Affairs. This is an example of close relationship that now exist between diplomacy and commerce.

The international intelligence agencies such as CIA of the USA, used to search for military secrets of other nations, but now they are engaged more in detecting industrial affair and up-to-date technologies. In the 1970s the Korean government was not willing develop diplomatic relationships with communist countries and even avoided those countries that have had diplomatic relationships with North Korea. This has been, however, radically changed. The Korean flag is now flying over Moscow, Beijing, and other capital cities of Eastern European countries. It does not matter with communists, liberals, democrats, or even the tyrannical. What matters is whether they have diplomatic relationships with other countries in order to sell their products to these countries.

A powerful nation used to mean a nation with a strong military, now it means a nation with strong economic power because the prices of up-to-date scientific weapons and research have gone sky high. Therefore, they cannot afford either to buy or produce weapons if they do not have the finical resources. In modern wars it is more important to have those scientific weapons than of having a large army fighting force. We have witnessed this in the Gulf War that the Iraqi soldiers of Saddam Hussein were captured in the dessert without shooting a single bullet. Why? Because they did not have the most current scientific weapons. Without economic power they will lose in modern warfare. Of course, they cannot be a powerful country without winning a victory in any warfare.

In his book, "The Rise and Fall of the Great Nations" Paul Kennedy, the famous professor of history at Yale University analyzed political structures of the great powers for the previous five centuries from the 17th century until now and concluded that the reason for the decrease in them was because they were not aware of the close relationships between military and economic power that the great powers tried to maintain their military power without any regard to economic support.

The Beginning of Economic Warfare

The white horse began to run in England, the red horse, in Russia, and the black horse started running in Europe. The European Community movement has already been proposed by many proponents.

Emmanuel Kant, a philosopher, proposed the Community Constitution in 1795. C. Saint Simon of France suggested to establish an European Parliament in 1848, and Victor Hugo of France proposed to establish a United States of Europe. In his writing, "Pan Occident" J. G. Fraser, an anthropologist, also insist states of Europe following the example of the USA.

In 1923, Coudenhove Kalergi of Australia also proposed to found an American style of the United States of Europe, and established a civil Pan-European community organization. European countries took a serious consideration on this idea right after World War II. They had more damage from the two world wars than ever before. If there would be another world war between the East and the West, it would probably be a nuclear war in Europe. Subsequently, the entire European continent would be destroyed.

After having a victory in the World War II Churchill, the Prime

Minister of Great Britain, proposed to establish United States of Europe on September 19, 1949.

Jean Monnet of France sponsored the European Community movement, so the issue had progressed. Jean Monnet was born in France in 1888 and worked his whole life for the French government. He served as a military officer in Algeria during World War II from 1943 till 1944 and came back to Paris with General De~Whene. When French soil were restored, he activated Churchill's proposal and played a central role in founding the European Community.

On June 25, 1950, the North Korean Army supported by USSR, crossed the Military Demarcation Line and attacked South Korea. The United Nation passed a resolution to send the UN Military Army to Korea for fighting against the North Korean Army. The winter of 1950, UN Army almost defeated the North Korea Army. Red China Army began to involve in the war. UN Military Army had to retreat from North Korea and USSR Air Force began to engage with US Air Force in the sky of Manchuria, China.

European nation's leaders began to worry about the expansion of the Korean War, that if Korean War would be expanded more it would be the Would War III, as the result European continent would fall into total ruins.

It was the Cold War Era, the NATO allied army power stand face to face to the Warsaw Communist Union Army in Europe. Even the Korean War did not expand to the Would War III, but possibly USA and USSR might fight against each other some time in the future. The future of Europe seems to be very dark.

How could not let that happen? There was only one solution, to forgive each other for the past conflicts among the European nations, to be united, and to have a good diplomatic relationships with both the USA and the USSR.

With this strategy, Jean Monnet promoted the European Community Movement by 1950. It was, however, realistic and reasonable that without economical independence and European political independence would not possible, therefore, they started to European Economic Community first.

European Economic Community Movement

I am going to describe the brief history of the European Economic Community Movement ;

On September 19, 1950 17 European countries which were members of the European Economic Cooperative Organization was established and the European Payment Union in order to provide payment and credit among the Western European countries.

In April 1951, the European Coal and Steel Community was established among France, Germany, Italy, and Benelux to break a trade wall and to build a community market. The general purpose for the community was for economic development, more employment, and better living through coal and steel production.

On March 25, 1957 they established the European Nuclear Energy Community(EURATOM) for providing the nuclear energy and using it for the peaceful peace, creating the necessary conditions to develop the relationships among member countries by providing good environment for development in order to build a community energy market, to supply the raw material, and to pursue a special plan for safe nuclear energy for human and environmental protection. While the US and the Soviet already have the nuclear weapons, if European nations do not have it they might have the problems on defense of Europe without nuclear weapon. By 1955 France and Great Britain developed and possessed the nuclear weapons because it would be difficult to be independent politically without it, even after European Union be established.

In the same year the European Economic Community was born as the result of the Roman Pact. This community was to establish a community market for the purpose of community economic, industrial, social, and financial strategies through allowing transferring merchandises, people, services, and capitals without restrictions. They decided in 1967 to put the three organizations EEC, ECSC and EURATOM under the control of European Community.

Since then the EC has developed rapidly. The European Summit meeting was officially formed in Paris on December 10, 1974. It became the official supreme organization and the European Parliament was organized in 1979.

On January 1st, 1993 after long run discussion the twelve countries together established the largest community market in the world. A free market exchanging merchandise, people, service, and capital in which includes 340 million population and 38 percent of the world gross interchange.

In January 1999 the European currencies unified and became an European Currency and began to use it by January 1, 2002. In the Fall of 1999 European Military General Headquarter was established and EU movement has been proceeded one more higher step.

There is a brief history of processing the European Community Movement:

Sep. 19, 1946 W. Churchill, the Prime Minister of Great Britain proposed the European Unification in Zurich

May. 27, 1951 Six countries joined the European Coal and Steel Community(ECSC)

Mar. 25 1957 The Roman Pact was signed for European Economic Community(EEC) and EURATOM

Mar. 19, 1958 Robert Schuman was elected as the Chairman of European Parliament

Nov. 20, 1959 European Free Trade Association(EFTA) was to be established

Nov. 1, 1964 The Korean Mission of the EC was established

Jul. 1, 1967 European Community was established that sets ECSC, EEC, and EURATOM under the control of EC

Mar. 1, 1975 The first European Summit meeting(the European Board of Directors) in Dublin, Ireland

Oct. 7, 1977 European Patent Office(EPO) was established in München June 16, 1979. The first 410 members of the European Parliament was elected.

(Dec. 27, 1979 The Soviet began to invade and attack Afghanistan)

(Sep. 22, 1980 the war between Iran and Iraq burst out)

Mar. 20, 1980 The first EC Cabinet meeting.

Jan. 1, 1985 The first European passport was issued.

(Apr. 15, 1988 the Soviet military began to withdraw from Afghanistan)

(May 30, 1988 president Reagan and Gorbachov of the Soviet Union jointly signed INF Treaty, and ended the Cold War)

(Nov. 9, 1989 The Berlin Wall down and started democratization movement in Eastern Europe)

May 29, 1990 FBRD was established to Eastern European economic reconstruction.

(Aug. 2, 1990 Iraq attacked Kuwait)

(Jan. 17, 1991 A multinational military attacked Iraq)

(Apr 1, 1991 Warsaw Pact was disorganized)

Mar. 1, 1993 ESM was established.

(Jan. 1, 1994 NAFTA was established by the USA, Canada and Mexico)

Jul. 30, 1995 EUROPOL was signed, be established.

Jan. 1, 1999 European currency was issued.

Jan. 1, 2002, European currency began to be used.

The World's Responses to the European Economic Community

As soon as the European Community Market was established to exchange their products without customs among the 12 European countries there were worldwide conflicts and problems in trading with European countries. It was obviously the USA faced the most big problems because the European countries were the major trading market of USA.

The economic war between the US and EC was largely expanded that President George Bush, the father of present President Bush organized North America Free Trading Association by Jan. 1st, 1994. NAFTA is also a giant organization which has around 38% of the would GDP. Since then Asian leaders also organized ASEAN and later Japan, Korea and China became the members so call ASEAN + Three were expanded and also Islam nations organized Islam Common Market.

There are four economic blocks in the world at the present time ; EFTA, NAFTA, ASEAN + 3, and ICM fighting against each other in this Economic War.

The Future of the Economic Warfare

We need to study carefully Revelation 6:6 to know the future of the economic warfare and will end.

"A quarter of wheat for day's wages, and three quarters of barley for day's wages."

One Denarius equals one day's wages at that time. It means that they can only buy a quarter of wheat or three quarters of barley with day's wages.

At the present time, one person can make at least $50 a day in USA which could buy about five sacks of wheat today, But the Bible said a quarter of wheat a day, that means the economic situation would become a problem. Why it will be happen?

It tells us two things:one is that monetary value will become low because of inflation and the grain price will go up due to famine. The other is economic panic will come because of high inflation. Worldwide economic depression is coming. Why? The book of Revelation tells the reason is because of the pale horse is coming. Which is energy war. Oil war is starting in the Middle East. It will be discussed in the next chapter

Prophecy of Hope

"Do not damage the oil and the wine"(Rev. 6:6).

The olive oil stands for "Spirit filled" and the wine is a symbol of "joy." Dr Sang Keun Lee interprets this verse, "(God) takes care of his children in the midst of tribulation and limit suffering." Many commentators interpret this verse as God's protection of his people in his mercy. During the economic warfare(the black horse), God will protect his children if they are filled with the Holy Spirit, full of joy, loving and obeying him, and faithfully working for the Great Commission.

How could the Spirit filled Christians be protected by God during the worldwide economic depression while others are suffering? I would like to answer this question as following. If we know, it is going to have rain today might prepare an umbrella that will be protected. Since Christians know the worldwide economic depression is coming so we would prepare the following things:

Let us prepare

What would we be prepare for the coming economic depression to be protected by God ?

1. Reduce monthly payments. If possible, pay off the debts reduce the payment. If you are running a business, try not to expand too large but to concentrate what you are doing safely.
2. Reduce credit card use as much as you could that has high interest rate.
3. Try to have a humble lifestyle, which is the Biblical.

Let us try to build up the credit in God

We believe in Jesus as our Savior who sacrificed himself for paying the price of our sins that I am not mine but his including my life, talent, time, house or car. Everything belongs to me is his. I am not an owner but a steward of him. Everything that we possess, money, honor, knowledge, experience, family is not ours but his because he purchased us at the cost of his own blood. We misunderstood that we are the owner of those things. We are niggardly offer to him, but waste money for ourselves. It is a sin.

Those who are filled with the Holy Spirit like olive oil and full of joy like wine must live as stewards. They are not stingy for the world mission but prudent for themselves. Our attitude toward money should be even when spending just one dollar ask, "Lord, may I spend your money for this?" When the Lord called us upon some day before him we are to report how we managed this money with empty hands. Those who are stewards will be protected by the Lord even the days of economic panic.

When Moses build up the credit in God even he and his people is the middle of the Sinai Desert where was no food and no water but God provided enough food and water from the rock. The King Ahab tried to find and kill the prophet Elijah so he had to hide near by Cherith Brook where was no food, but God supplied the feed for him through ravens because of Elijah's credit in God. The widow didn't have any food for three and half years famine but God supplied her enough flour and oil.

"Do not damage the oil and the wine"(Rev. 6:6).

It is a command of God who is able and almighty. He commanded the world to be created that will be fulfilled when we obey him for his glory.

The Economic Warfare and the Providence of God

Why did God allow us to have the Economic Warfare? What might be the providence of God in this Economic War era? The answer is clear.

God wanted to end of the Red Horse era which was the Communist Revolutionary Ideological War era, another word, Cold War era. Why?

There are two reasons to fulfill the prophecy of Jesus in Matthew 24:14 and Luke 21:29-31. God has given us the last chance to witness Jesus even to the former communist nations. If Jesus come back to us before the Communist nations fall it might be impossible to have the judgment to the young people in those nations because the young people in the communist nations never hear of the Gospel.

And the second reason is to fulfill the prophecy of Jesus in Luke 21:29-31. The small and the weak races and nations have to be independent.

The Miracle Year, 1989

The year of 1989 can be called "the Year of a Miracle." As the result of the democratic revolution in Eastern Europe the strong communist governments in Poland, Hungary, Czechoslovakia and Rumania collapsed. In November the Berlin Wall was destroyed and in October of the next year the Eastern and Western Germany were reunited. These events were the signals of transformation of history, the end of the Cold War and beginning of the Post Cold War era.

It would be impossible to happen this miracle without the new leader of the Soviet Union, Mikhail Gorbachev. He was inaugurated as the Chief Secretary of the Soviet Communist Party in 1985 as the first leader of the post revolution generation. He declared Perestroika(reconstruction) and Glasnost(openness) as the foundation of political policies, bringing up a worldwide ripple.

M. Gorbachov embodied the democratization, economic system reform, and cultural and art freedom by political liberalization policy. He tried to report in newspapers for the bureaucratic corrupts, social absurdness, and political mistakes so that his reform would contribute to reestablish economical power and to restore the international leadership.

On the one hand he shunned military expense competition against the USA and tried to change the Soviet economic system from military centered industry to consumer goods centered industry. Thus, he made so called the INF Provisional Treaty with the USA in Washington in 1987(a treaty to withdraw and dissolve the short distance nuclear missile from Europe and Asia and to supervise military leaders of both nations). The INF Treaty was signed by President Reagan and Gorbachov in May 1988 and it began to be effective by June 1, 1988.

On August 23, 1989 1 million people of the three ethnic groups in Baltic area Estonia, Latvia, and Lithuania made a 620 km human chain and protested against Germany-Soviet Nonaggression Treaty that was made between Stalin and Hitler about 50 years ago. As a result, the three groups declared their independence.

In march 1991, Sovereign Republic Federation Treaty was passed by 76% of absolute large number through a national vote and Yeltsin became the President of Russia. Gorbachev issued a new federation treaty, modifying as Republic Union and tried to maintain the Soviet Union. However a coup detat broke out. On September 21 they joined on a parliamentary policy to establish the CIS. On 25th day of that month, Gorbachev resigned the presidency, and the Soviet Union was broken after 63 years' reign. Therefore, all small ethnic groups under the control of the Soviet Union could be independent.

Now, we need to ascertain the reason why God brought up Economic Warfare. The prophecy of Luke 21:29-31 was finally fulfilled through independence of small nations under the Soviet Union. Let us remember the verse:"when these things begin to take place, stand up and lift up your heads, because your redemption is drawing near"(Luke. 21:28). "when you see these things happening, you know that the kingdom of god is near" (Luke. 21:31).

What are "these things?" As it have mentioned earlier, it is the complete fulfillment of Luke 21:28-31. As the chief communist country, the Soviet Union was collapsed, the other small ethnic groups have been independent. We did not anticipate the Soviet

Union will be collapsed. The prophecy of the text was fulfilled partially in the western world during the Cold War era. However, it completely fulfilled in this generation. It is the second wake up call from God.

Why does God want us to wake up spiritually? If one is in spiritual sleep, cannot attain the mission. Lift up your eyes and look at the world. The door is widely open to the all of the Communist countries, even Soviet and Red China today. We had never dreamed about this era 10 years ago.

Isn't this dreamy reality? God is eager to see us waking up and doing the final task to fulfill the prophecy in Matthew 24:14. Listen those who have the ears and the raising and fall of all nations are according to the providence of God.

Chapter 10
Opening the Fourth Seal
(Islam Revolution War)

"When the lamb opened the fourth seal, I heard the voice of the fourth living creature say, 'Come!' I looked, and there before me was a pale horse! Its rider was named Death, and Hades was following close behind him. They were given power over a fourth of the earth to kill by sword, famine and plague, and by the wild beasts of the earth"(Rev. 6:7-8, NIV).

Interpreting this passage is very difficult.

Textual Analysis

The appearance of a pale horse means after the economic war there would be another war. "Pale" signifies the color of death ; in this period many people would die physically and spiritually. The name of the rider was "Death" and "Hades", that is, "Hell" was following. The rider must not be a political leader but a religious leader, for people do not go to hell as a result of following any political leader. Only the anti-Christ or heretic leaders could lead people to hell. Because the rider's name was Death, it must be a kind of cult of the lifeless anti-Christ which entices people with dead theology into hell. They have great power because they were given power over a fourth of the earth. The four kinds of weapons that the rider uses:

Sword:political and military power
Famine:The rider would use a weapon bring famine
Plague:In Greek, *thavatos*, meaning an epidemic
Beasts:a weapon of cruelty

In conclusion, the rider of a pale horse has following four elements:

He/she is the anti-Christ under Satan's power that leads people to the hell. He/she has power over a fourth of the earth.
He/she is cruel enough to kill many people.
He/she would bring a big change in climate.

What is the possible interpretation of the power over a fourth of the earth about?

1. One fourth of the entire land.
2. One fourth of the world population.
3. One fourth of the world products.

4. One fourth of the world nations.

Let us examine those possibilities.

One fourth of the whole land

It is possibly true. If this was a period of colonialism it would be possible to conquer one fourth of land of the earth, but the colonial period has passed by. After the World War II almost all small nations have become independent. They do not dream of the conquest the world like Napoleon or colonialism any more because it is impossible. The colonial period, the age of white horse, has passed by. The fourth horse signifies another war after the economic war. Therefore, it is not quite right to interpret this as one fourth of entire land.

One fourth of the world population

This option came to be possible in the late twentieth century. It was never before that one nation had one fourth of whole world population. After 1970s however, the population of China has been over 1 billion, which is about one fourth of the world population.

Nobody knows if a leader like the anti-Christ comes from China to cause people to go to hell. It seems impossible now because the current China is namely communists' country, but it is becoming capitalistic economic system. It might be impossible for China to maintain it's current population unless she keeps opening her system to economic development. It is only possible to cooperate with the western democratic countries in order to open politics and economic development. If she oppresses religious freedom and human rights, cooperation with the western countries will be impossible.

One fourth of the world products

The entire products of the USA sums one fourth of the world products. The EU(European Union) also has the similar amount of products as the USA. It seems impossible to rise an anti-Christ in these two areas because of long lasting influence of Christianity and a developed democracy. People could be deceived if they had not tasted freedom, but it cannot be imagined to accept an anti-Christ in these areas.

One fourth of the world allied-nations

We have seen diverse allies among nations in modern history such as NATO, a military ally, European Community, an economic alley, and geographical allies. As it is mentioned above, the characteristics of the one fourth of the world allied-nations in the text are following:

1. A religious community which has political and military power.
2. Against Christianity and anti-Christ.
3. Mass-killing.
4. Brings famines.

This community must appear after 1950 when the economic war

started.

What is this community? The possible religious communities are Christianity, Buddhism, Taoism, Judaism, Islam and Hinduism. Buddhism, Hinduism, Taoism, and Judaism exist only in a number of areas, and Christianity does not separate a nation from politics and tries to grab national power. The only possibility falls on to the Islam. Islam is a religion and political power at the same time. Now the number has expanded to 55 nations, which is over one fourth of entire nations. Therefore, it is reasonable to interpret that the rider of the pale horse is the Islam.

In 1991, George Otis Jr. published a book titled, "The Last of the Giants", in which he describes the Islamic movement. He describes in detail about Islamic revolution led by Ayatollah Ruhollah Khomeini and how the evil spirit behind Islam led the young to cruel and horrible results. Modern Christians should read this book to know our enemies.

Samuel Huntington, a political science scholar and professor of Harvard University, published a book, "Clash of Civilizations and the Remaking of the World Order" in 1997. His book is excellent. He analyzes today's world in a political sense, explaining that the world is rushing to a clash of civilizations after the secession of the Cold War. He thinks that the last war would break out by clashing western civilization against Asian civilization.

The Islamic Resurgence

In his book Huntington describes the Islamic resurgence (ch. 3 pt 5, p. 109).

In the early 1970s the oil price was increasing so the Islamic nations have accumulated enormous wealth and power from fluctuations in oil price. They started despising Christianity and showing off Islamic superiority. They have insisted on accepting modernization, yet reject western culture, remaining in or returning to Islam as a right political, social, religious decision. Therefore, the Islamic resurgence is not merely religious movement but political, social, and a cultural movement. They have a belief that the answer for all the problems in the world is Islam. They reject people's nation, yet their branches vary from modern reformers to violent revolutionaries, similar to Marxism.

The Islamic strategies always start with social welfare, dealing with isolated and poor people in a society. They expand their power by building relief agencies, clinics, hospitals, and schools. In the USA Islam had started with black low-income communities and now there are over 5 million Muslims. They have spread the Islamic belief from social welfare and culture to politics and society as a whole. Especially, Islam has expanded its influence to public schools. Alumni from those schools organize students' rallies, youth organizations, religious, societal, and educational associations. Therefore, the core power in Islam major's young students and intellects that have been brought up in the process of modernization. They appeal more to students from technical, engineering, and scientific colleges. When they reach to some point in terms of the Islamic population they start anti-government movement and then overthrow a government to take political power. Today, the increase rate of natural population of Islam is the highest in the world, and it is increasing rapidly.

Islamic Weapons

There appear four kinds of weapons in the text.

The "sword"

A sword signifies military and political power. Around 1973, during the higher oil price and the Gulf War, the Islamic countries purchased a lot of weapons and have been gaining political power after then. When an Islamic country is invaded, all Islamic countries cooperate to defeat.

For example, when the USSR attacked Afghanistan in December 1979, all Islamic countries banded together, defeated the USSR and won the war. Finally, the USSR military withdrew from Afghanistan in 1988. Of course, the USA also supported the war ; especially with the Stinger missile which was an important factor to help win. Most importantly, however, the entire Islamic countries cooperated to win the war. Saudi Arabia gave 3 billion dollars, and Islamic countries sent 25,000 soldiers. Pakistan also provided military training and a supply base. They also supported Kosovo in Yugoslavian civil war, and now they help International Islamic in Chechen.

At the Gulf War, Iran, Jordan, Libya, Mauritania, Yemen, Sudan, and Tunisia supported Iraq. Sadam Hussein stated that the USA and western Christian countries tried to obliterate the Islam through the war. The Islam was influenced by a hostile feeling against the USA, praising Hussein as their hero. They saw Hussein as a cruel dictator and his attack to Kuwait as wrong decision, yet impeached the USA's intervention, insisting it was still a problem of Arab. They were proud that they won the battle against the USSR during the Afghanistan Civil War and dared to challenge the USA, the last super-power.

Pakistan has recently possessed nuclear weapons and its carrier and other Islamic countries, Iran, Libya, and Algeria want to have nuclear weapons, too. They have been convinced that because Israel has nuclear weapons they should also have nuclear capabilities. They are now developing long-distance missiles.

The "Sword", military and political power of Islam has been increased. From these historical evidences, we know that the prophecies in the Book of Revelation will become true.

Famine

The second weapon is famine.

"There will be famines and earthquakes in various places" (Matt. 24:7).

"There will be earthquakes in various places, and famines" (Mk. 13:8).

"There will be great earthquakes, famines, and pestilences"

(Lk. 21:11).

Above are signs of the End of the Day written in Jesus prophecies. At the End of the Day there will be bad years, and consequently will be famines all over the world. There have been famines many places in the world since 1990. Why does it become more serious problems recently? What causes famines?

El Nino, name of a southward-flowing ocean current off the cost of Peru, brings an extraordinary phenomenon to climatic change, floods, famines, and bad crops. In 1993, the Mississippi River was overflowed its banks because of the El Nino, covering up the city and damaging crops. In 1995, El Nino again brought northern California and Europe huge floods. There was snow at the Golan Heights which was very rare, covering up with snow about 1 meter. In the desert areas such as Jordan, Syria, and Israel had to close the roads because of unexpected snow. In Amman, the capital of Jordan, there was over 40 cm snow on the other hand some areas like Korea and other places had to limit city water because of drought.

"El Nino" means "Baby Jesus" in Spanish. Because El Nino usually comes at Christmas season, it was named as such. El Nino brings extraordinary climatic changes world widely because of the unusual current of the Pacific Ocean, which causes 7-8 degrees higher temperature than normal. It comes cyclic and brings disasters. It comes with storms, heavy rains, and drought, causing large damages to crops, and accordingly, the price goes up higher. It brings Asian countries summer cold and continental high temperature, which result in enormous damages. In the early 1995, while I was writing this, El Nino came and brought Europe and California winter floods, and Korea and Japan drought.

Scientists insist that the oil is the principal on the global worming. When we use the oil, a lot of Carbon dioxide come out by burning oil and making the climatic changes and the air pollution.

Islam would use the famine as the weapon which means to use the oil weapon.

The environmental movement

Oil is necessary product in modern society, and at the same time it is the chief reason for air pollution. Between 1960 and early1970 there had been an environmental movement in the USA demanding "clean air, clean water." As a result, their establishment of the Department of Environment and the government began to control it to protect and provide clean air and water. Because coal is the worst in polluting the air the industrial circles began to use heavy oil. Consequently, the oil demand increased which pressed the oil market greatly and fastened the energy crisis in 1973.

After the energy crisis, western industrial countries started building atomic power stations to produce energies to overcome the crisis and to avoid environmental pollution. There happened, however, a terrible accident. In April 1986, from an atomic power station in Chernobyl, Ukraine, radioactivity was flown out. This radioactivity flied to Europe by wind. The European countries detected the radioactivity. When they asked the USSR about it at the first time, they denied the fact. In a few days, however, reports arrived to Moscow of a revolt at a railroad station in Kiev, massive refugees and deaths caused by the disaster. The western countries began to criticize the USSR, and finally, Gorbachov admitted the accident on TV after two weeks. A politician analyzed that incident was the decisive chance to open the USSR its door.

In the USA, there was a similar accident on Three-Mile Island, so every body was evacuated. So the environmental movement is not limited to one nation any more ; it is a worldwide issue. Thus, there was an international symposium for the issue in 1992.

After the oil crisis in 1973, countries started investing large amount of money to develop alternative energies. The research and development has been going on in the USA such as windmill energy, solar energy system, tide energy development, terrestrial heat energy, and so on, but it has not been successful enough to develop an alternative to oil energy.

It is reported that the atomic energy is most economic so far, yet it accompanies great risk to use. Those accidents in Chernobyl or Three-Mile Island proved the danger. The recent report tells us that one out of hundred children has cancer after Chernobyl radioactive leaking accident. Thus, the protectionists of environment oppose against the building of atomic energy power plants with worldwide organizations. As a result, oil is still at the throne of energy until it runs out.

The demand for oil will be increasing continuously, which resulted in air pollution and becomes a serious problem. The more air polluted, the worse El Nino becomes. The Jet Propel Lab(JPL) under the NASA and France have recently launched a satellite, Tofax-Poseidon, together and analyzed the collected data. They found out that the recent El Nino was stronger than before. The speaker of the JPL said that El Nino came more often than before. It happened once every five or seven year, then every three or five year, and now it happens every other year.

The Place of Oil in the Modern World

Daniel Yergin, the director of Energy Research Institute of Cambridge University, Massachusetts, published a book, "The Prize" in 1990. He did an excellent work in the book, a historical study on oil power in the modern society. Paul Kennedy insists, "the rise and fall of the great power is on its economic power", yet Yergin says that it is not economy but energy that handles the rise and fall of the great powers, becoming a powerful weapon.

It is a historical fact that oil brought capitalism and modern industrial society, becoming the center of development. Oil industries appeared at the end of nineteenth century and have developed for ten years enormously. Oil companies came to the world as international enterprises and started controlling the world economy by management strategies, innovating technologies, and marketing.

Those who control oil, control the world. Oil has been one of the most crucial strategic goods since World War Ⅱ. Oil made the decision who won and lost the battle at the World War Ⅱ. After Japan attacked Pearl Harbor, the first places she conquered were southeastern islands such as Borneo and Java where oil was produce. The reason Germany attacked Russia first was to occupy the Caucasus oil fields. At the end of the war, the oil tanks of Japan and Germany were almost empty, so they ran on charcoal.

One of the important factors contributing to the USA winning the war was to secure oil. During the era of the Cold War, the Great Powers continued to control oil-producing countries secretly. The Suez Canal crisis ended up the colonialism of old Europe. Those countries that control oil have become wealthy, and because of oil the industrially advanced nations continue economic development.

Oil is like gold, weapon, and the artery of life. We cannot live a day without oil. Because of that, some anthropologists call modern people oil people. Oil is the artery of civil life and indispensable element. It is also provides raw material for chemical fertilizer, controlling modern agriculture. It provides not only fuels for carrying crops from farms to cities but also necessary element for plastics and industrial products. Modern civilization depends on oil.

Oil, however, has become the principal offender of polluting the air, so it has become the target of environment protectionists. If we no longer neither uses no vehicles that run on oil nor run factories that use oil. These are the major factors polluting the air. Yet, because the demand of oil increases yearly, environmental problems become more serious. Compare to the early 1990, the world population has increased about twenty percents at the end of 1990s. As the population grows, so do the products and pollution.

Now, we begin to understand what it means that the weapons of the rider of the pale horse can be famine and drought. Their great power comes from oil. Most Islamic countries have oil. It has been a long time that they have used the sword of oil, but we encountered its seriousness in 1973, the year of oil crisis.

I have come to a conclusion in interpreting those horses, that the white horse is the mission movement of Christianity through colonialism, the red horse is ideological war, that is, communists' movement, the black horse which had scale is economic war started with European Community, and the pale horse is energy war, began with Islamic movement.

The Rise of Oil Weapon

As I mentioned above, the modern industrial society cannot live without oil. Oil, however, cannot be produced anywhere like agricultural or industrial products. Its amount is also limited. Therefore, the oil producing countries make use of it as political, diplomatic, economic, and military power.

Daniel Yergin describes in his book, "The Prize" the oil crisis in 1973 as the "oil weapon." Let us discuss about the history and process of the oil conflicts.

The First Oil Crisis(1951)

Yergin insists that the oil crisis began when Mohammad Mossadegh tried to nationalize the Anglo-Iranian oil company in 1950. Mossadegh was the Chairman of the Oil Committee of the Iranian Congress. He spoke at the Congress that they should nationalize the Anglo-Iranian oil company because they had 51 percents of entire stocks but the Prime Minister, Razmara opposed to him in 1951. The radicals of Islam assassinated Razmara, insisting to kill the spy of the Great Britain was a holy mission. After a week, they killed the Minister of Education, too. In April 1951, they nationalized the Anglo-Iranian oil company and elected Mossadegh as the Prime Minister. Mossadegh legalized the nationalization, and sent the governor of the state to Kuzistan, where the main office of the oil company was located with the seal and signboard.

Great Britain tried to compromise to share the half of the benefit, but it was not successful. Mr. Harriman of the USA also tried to intervene, but failed. Then Britain wanted to send the military to resolve the problem, but the USA did not agree because of the possibility of the World War III caused by the USSR. At the same time, it was right after the Korean War in which the USA had sacrificed its armies and soldiers a great deal.

The nationalization of Anglo-Iranian Oil Company has become a model case for many Middle Eastern countries to try the same thing.

The Second Oil Crisis(1956)

The Suez Canal incident in 1956 was the second oil crisis. Suez Canal, a 100 mile-waterway between the Mediterranean Sea and the Red Sea, was built in the nineteenth century by Ferdrando de Lessepe of France. It was thought to be impossible to construct the waterway, so when it was done it was considered to be one of the greatest constructional technologies in the nineteenth century. It construction started in 1859 and finished in 1869.

France owned a half of all stocks and operated the waterway, while the British wished to use it because it was a shortcut for a merchant ship sailing from India. It is about 11,000 miles form India around the Cape of Good Hope to Britain, but it is just 6,500 miles through Suez Canal. The time of fortune came in 1875 ; the Khedive, the ruler of Egypt was about to bankrupt. Britain bought 44 percents of stocks from Egypt, and after that both France and Britain operated the Canal together. After the World War II, the European industries were revived and two thirds of whole cargo was oil-transporting ships. It became like an artery of Europe ; and two thirds of entire oil used in Europe was carried through Suez Canal.

In 1952, however, Colonel Gamal Abdel Nasser of Egypt carried out a military coup and he expelled the General Mohammed Naigai and became an Egyptian tyrant.

He advocated Arabian nationalism and to expel the Jews from Middle East and to destroy Israel. He opened a radio station, "Arabian Voice", and continued to stir up entire Arabian countries.

Though he became a ruler of Egypt, he lacked experiences. He thought that if the country nationalized the Suez Canal, they would develop nation's economy, so he intrigues the USSR in his plan and integrated them into the United Arab States. The USSR provided Egypt with a large amount of weapon. Nasser began to dream of having control over the world with oil by using it as weapon ; he thought that the western industrial nations would be destroyed without oil. Thus, Nasser tries to nationalize Suez Canal. Knowing this, Eaton, the Prime Minister of Great Britain, tried to compromise the problem by withdrawing British military from the Canal, but it was not successful. France and Britain saw the problem just as Hitler moved into Finland, violating the public international law, so they decided to resolve the problem by military forces.

President Eisenhower also saw this crisis seriously, so held an urgent committee to resolve the problem. He let the committee examine alternative ways to supply oil to European countries when their ships could not pass through Suez Canal. One of the alternatives that the committee examined was to build an underground oil transport system from Iraq through Turkey. It took, however, four years to build, and cost about $400,000,000, so it was not able to alleviate the problem.

On 24th of October 1956, the Ministers of Foreign Affairs, staffs, and military leaders from the UK, France, and Israel gathered together in Savres, suburb of Paris, and had a secret meeting to discuss united operations. The plan was about to expel

Nasser by occupying the Sinai Peninsula by Israel and being stationed in Suez Canal by the UK and France after sending a final note to Nasser. On the same day of the meeting in Savres, however, the USSR invaded Hungary, killing those who cried out for freedom from being controlled by the USSR

To make matters worse, the two headships of the USA and the UK were ill:Eaton, the Prime Minister of the UK was in bed after a herniptomy and Eisenhower was in recovery from a heart attack and bypass surgery. Because of the situation, they spent several months without any decision-making.

Finally, Israel started attacking the Egyptian military in Sinai Peninsula on 29 October 1956. France and the UK sent a final note on October 30th, and dropping bombs to the Egyptian airport on 31st. That made the USA raged. After the World War II, the USA has supported Europe like a friend, forming the North Atlantic Treaty Organization. Especially, the USA might have felt betrayed by the UK, which was like the best friend. It was a critical time to help Hungarian innocent free civilians from the massacre done by the USSR military, yet the UK and France began battles in the Sinai and Suez Canal. The critical point was that there might be a possibility for the Arabian oil producing countries to close oil-export. Furthermore, the USSR would expand its power by providing Middle Eastern Arabian countries weapons. There was also a possibility to have a third World War. If the USSR would grab hegemony to the Middle East, it would give the USA and other western countries harmful influences. Therefore, the USA did not want to turn away from the Middle Eastern oil producing countries.

Eisenhower was outraged when he heard the news while he was involved in presidential campaigning in southern areas. He himself made a phone call to Eaton and criticized him badly, but it was Eaton's aide who received the call.

It is said that stationing at the Suez Canal by the UK and French military was delayed because of Eaton's illness and his inability to make an immediate determination. It was this delay that allowed Nasser to cover the Suez Canal by bombing a ship filled with rocks, loads of cement, and empty bottles, so the Canal was closed and no oil ships sailed from Middle East to Europe. That caused a tremendous trouble to Europe, because of amount of oil leftover. Three fourth of the oil carried to Europe was cut out. They were not able to live out the winter unless the USA provided oil. As they anticipated, Saudi Arabia forbade exporting oil to the UK and France, and made Kuwait's supply system stop. The oil prices suddenly jumped in the UK and France. Accordingly, the market price rose up, and stock price fell down ; an economic crisis occurred. The UK asked for urgent economic support to IMF, but was rejected because she failed to get agreement from the USA.

Meanwhile, it was told that the USA might forbid exporting oil to Europe. Eisenhower strongly opposed against supplying Europe oil saying, "Those who make a problem solve it." Finally, France and the UK yielded to the USA, and withdrew their military from Egypt and replaced them to the United Nations' army. After that, Eisenhower summoned the National Security Committee and examined the possibility of sending an oil supply to Europe. Finally, they decided to carry oil directly from the USA across the Atlantic Ocean. When the USA oil-ships arrived at European harbors, the OEEC took responsibility to distribute it to each country. Therefore, the second oil crisis was ended in 1957. This oil transporting strategy was successful, so they were able to supply 90 percent of what was lacking. In March 1957, part of the Iraqi oil transporting pipes started operating, and in April of the same year they removed obstacles out of the way from Suez Canal so that they could cross the Canal. Thereafter, the Suez Canal has belonged to Egypt, and the USA closed the emergent oil supply strategy.

Though they were powerful countries in Europe, the UK and France learned a lesson through their own history about Suez Canal that they would not be a powerful nations without oil. A year this incident the London Times critiqued, "The Prime Minister Eaton was the last one who believed that Great Britain was the power of the world."

The Third Oil Crisis (1967)

The successful nationalization of oil brought Nasser self-indulgence. They do not claim oil as weapon, because Egypt does not produce oil, yet their military force has a strong power. They tried to destroy Israel. In May 1957, they forced the United Nation military to withdraw from Egypt, and placed their own army in

Sinai Peninsula.

Nasser had Syria, an allied country, to terrorize Israel and put Jordan's military under his command. He closed the Agapa Gulf to blockade Israel's route for oil transportation. They planned to let all the Arabian countries in the Middle East send their armies. On June fourth, Egypt and Jordan issued a military pact. Israel was about to be besieged by Arabian countries.

Israel was watching and analyzed Nasser's plot, and made a judgment on Nasser's attack to Israel. Israel, therefore, started striking first on June 5th. This was the beginning of the Six-Day Battle. In a several hours, Israel defeated the Egyptian and Arabian Air force and advanced to the Sinai Peninsula, destroying the Egyptian army. On June 8th, they marched to Suez Canal. About 80 percent of Egyptian army was defeated. On the third day, Israel military marched to Jordan and Syria, and they withdrew from the battlefields without fighting. Israel won the battle after six days, and ceased firing.

On June 6, the second day of the battle, Arabian Ministers of oil affairs prohibited to export oil to Israel's allied nations such as the USA, the UK, and Western Germany. Yamani of Saudi Arabia warned Amoco Oil Company that no more oil shipments should be sent to the USA. The reason for this was namely to show Arabian unity, but the real reason for this was that they had several nationwide problems:strikes of the laborers, riots, violence, and political crises. They reduced oil production to 40 percent from June 8th, and the Abidjan Oil Company of Iran was closed. Arabian oil supply reduced 600 barrel per day. The Oil crisis in 1967 was much more serious than that in 1956. To make the matter worse there was civil war in Nigeria, one of the oil producing countries, and the USA was involved in the Vietnam War.

President Johnson established a special committee in Europe for oil supply, and appointed Mr. George Bundy as the chairman to set up a consistent policy. He had 24 oil companies in the USA attend the committee and told them to supply oil to the allied nations. The Suez Canal was closed and Iraqi pipeline were also closed so the only way to supply oil to Europe was through the Cape of Good Hope of Africa.

They built six huge oil ships, which were seven times bigger than those used in Suez Canal crisis eleven years earlier, but they were transporting between the Middle East and Europe. So the problem was lack of oil ships. Fortunately, the problems of each country had been resolved, so the oil crisis was quickly settled down. Those who lost their benefits from this crisis were the countries that participated in embargo oil exporting. They had to go through economic difficulties. Finally, the oil embargo was released in September of the same year. The oil producing countries competed to increase the amount of production. Accordingly, the oil price went down because the supply exceeded the need.

Chumacher, an economist and writer for the Times and the Economies said, "There is no alternative to energy. Every area of modern life has been founded on energy. Energy is not a merchant, buying or selling like other goods. It is a most basic and necessary thing like air and water. Energy is the foundation of all material."

Weaponization of Oil

The Fourth Oil Crisis(1973, the 4th Middle Eastern War)

It was Yom Kippur, the Day of Atonement, the most important holiday of Israel October 6, 1973. Everybody from highest government official and generals to people prepared for celebrating on that day. It was about 2 o'clock at night when the Egyptian air force started firing on Israeli headquarters and military base in Sinai. Syrian fighters started firing at military facilities on borders of northern Israel. This was beginning the 4th Middle Eastern War, called October Battle. It was the most destructive battle of all the wars in Middle East. The two powers, the USA and the USSR provided weapons for the war and the oil was used as weapon.

The Egyptian and Syrian armies were armed with most recent weapons supplied form the USSR and they took advantage of containment offensive. Two days after the surprise attack, Mose Dayan, the Minister of National Defense of Israel reported to Golda Meir, the Premier, that the third battle line had almost fallen. Israel urgently asked president Nixon in Washington for help.

Signs of the War

In June 1973 Brezhnev, the Chairman of Secretaries of the USSR visited President Richard Nixon of the USA. Nixon invited him to his villa in Sacramento, California. Breaking the diplomatic custom, Brezhnev asked Nixon to talk. The two heads of state had three and half hour-long talk that night in Nixon's small library. Brezhnev foretold Nixon that there would be a war in Middle East before long, and shared his hope of peace between their two countries. Nixon and Kissenger, the National Defense Aide, interpreted this as warning against Middle East, and as the USSR taking the initiative in resolving the Middle Eastern problems.

On August 23, 1973, President Sadat of Egypt visited Liyadh, the capital city of Saudi Arabia, without telling anyone and had a secret meeting with the King Faisal. He declared a war against Israel and asks for war expenses, so King Faisal promised 500 million dollars. He also asked permission to use oil as a weapon. The king suggested a prolonged war in order that oil-weapon would be more effective because they needed time to rise public opinion in using oil-weapon. On August 27, the king had a meeting with the Oil Minister, Yamani and ask to have a weekly report from the Armaco Oil Company, and at the same time, he made a strong comment on the US policy toward Israel, criticizing it. That was another sign of the war.

About two or three weeks before the surprising attack, the US got a report from a Syrian intelligence agent that they were building a huge base with all kinds of Syrian fighters. They also obtained information on the movement of the Egyptian military and on the emptying space of hospital bed of Egyptian hospitals. The National Security Council of the USA let the CIA agents to analyze this information. They reported that there would not be a possibility of a war but a seasonal training of Egyptian military. Later, it was proved that the report was true.

One of the first lieutenants of Israel reported an impending war, watching the relocating of the Egyptian army between October 1st and 3rd, but it was ignored. Another intelligence agency from Egypt sent a report of impending war, but it was also not accepted. When Israel was attacked surprisingly, it had the same shock factor as the Pearl Harbor attack by Japan.

Weapon Supply by the USA and the USSR

The USSR publicly started supply the retreating Syrian military with weapons and ammunition, and they encouraged Arabian countries to become involved in the war, trying to take control of the Middle East. Whoever seized Middle East could grasp oil, and that means taking over the world. That is why the USA would not give in to the Middle East or the USSR. The USA started to transport weapons and ammunition by Israeli airplanes. They also tried to rent civil aviation to supply weapons, but none would send their planes to the battlefields. If the President declared a national emergency they could be compelled to use planes, but it would not be in the case of a war between Israel and Arab. The USA was in dilemma:if they publicly supply Israel weapons and ammunition, then the Arabian countries would prohibit oil-exportation ; if not, one of the allied nations would be destroyed by the USSR.

On October 12th, President Nixon received two letters. One was from Meir, the Prime Minister of Israel, an SOS asking for urgent help. The other from the Presidents of four oil companies, Exxon, Texaco, Mobil, and California Standard, telling him that the Arabian oil countries would increase oil price up to 100 percent and that if the USA gave Israel military support the Arabs in revenge would and might embargo oil-export. President Nixon fell in dilemma.

Kissinger commanded Schlesinger, the Minister of National Defense, to use military planes. On October 14, a formation of C5A, transport planes of the US airborne troops filled with war supplies took off from midwestern base toward Tel Aviv airport in Israel. They, however, needed gas on the way. They landed on Lajes airfield in the Azores, Portugal for gas, and flew on to Tel Aviv. They arrived at the Tel Aviv airport at night, dropping off war supplies and back to the USA at dawn. They continued to supply Israel with weapons and ammunition.

Arabian countries finally knew about the US secret transporting of war supplies. Through this action, the USA made sure that she keeps trust with her friendly nations at any cost.

Arabian Revenge

On October 16th, five Arabian countries made a decision to

increase oil price up to 70 percent, which was the first decision -making on oil-price. The next day, Nixon summoned the National Security Counsel to discuss Arabian strategy of using oil as a weapon. The US needed negotiation. The agenda was to suggest ceasing the war, making reconciliation according to the UN Resolution 242 stating that Israel would withdraw her boarder back to that border before 1967, and Arabs would consent to it. Nixon was positive on this resolution, so he summoned his cabinet to explain on October 18th. He declared to supply weapons to Israel because the USSR tried to take control over the Middle Eastern oil field by supplying the Arabs with mass weapons. The next day, he suggested to support Israel with 22,000 million dollars.

On hearing this, Libya declared to prohibit oil-export to the USA. On October 20th Saudi Arabia, which was relatively closer to the USA also declared embargo. Nine Arabian Ministers of oil had a secret meeting and decided to decrease oil production down to 5 percent per month, and to prohibit oil-export to the USA. Now, oil became like a general over a war.

In the meantime, the Israel army succeeded in making a counterattack on the Egyptian army before they went through mountain road at Sinai. They continued to pursuit and surrounded the Egyptian Third Army Corps. For the Egyptian army, they would either have to be annihilated or captured.

On October 20, when Kissinger was in a plane flying toward Moscow to negotiate with Arabs he heard two surprising things on the news:one was the Saudi Arabian embargo and the other was about the Watergate scandal. Nixon faced three critical issues :Middle Eastern war, oil-embargo, and the Watergate. After that day, Kissinger took charge of all the diplomatic issues and Nixon dealt with his own problem with the Watergate scandal.

The USSR did not just sit and watch the Egyptian Third Army be annihilated. Brezhnev sent Nixon a challenging letter, "… the USSR would not sit and look on while the Egyptian Third Army Corps would be destroyed who were fighting with the USSR weapons. If so, we would lose credits. Let us stop the war by sending united army from both USSR and the USA. If the USA would not approve, we will send our troops." The US military informers received information that the USSR airborne corps was waiting, the USSR fleet was moving from the Mediterranean Sea toward Sinai Peninsula, and they found a nuclear waste leaking from an USSR cargo ships, which proved that they loaded nuclear weapons on the ships.

The US National Security Counsel had an emergency meeting at night to consider a counterplan, and decided to fight against power with power. On October 25th in the morning, they commanded the US military over the world to warn against nuclear war. That was the first crisis between the USA and the USSR after the Cuban crisis. It was a world crisis, the threat of being destroyed by a nuclear war. Fortunately, the next day the Middle Eastern war was ceased, and the Egyptian Third Army Corps got supplies. Two days later, the two representatives from both Israel and Egyptian armies met together to talk ; it was the first talk within a quarter of century. The USA and Egypt also opened a channel to talk. The Arabian oil-embargo, however, was continued.

Influence of Oil Weapon

The oil war in 1973 had a worldwide influence.

Wade of Worldwide Depression

Arabian oil countries increased oil price with their own right in 1973. The agreed price on October 16 was $5.40. In November Nigerian oil was $16 and in December Iranian oil was $17, which was as much as six times the amount than before the war. One of the Japanese companies was criticized because it's bid for oil pricing was up to $22.60. The oil price had continuously increased :$1.80 in 1970 ; $2.18 in 1971 ; $2.90 in 1972 ; $5.12 in May 1973 ; $11.65 in December 1973.

Decreasing oil production brought increasing oil prices and higher price resulted in enormous rise in price of commonalities. Because oil is a necessary good in modern industry, the rise of price was inevitable. Producing goods in factories, transporting those goods, public transportation, and civic home life are all influenced by oil. Oil price had a huge economic impact on modern industrial nations' deadlock in economic growth, withdraws in business, inflation, damages in international stock markets, and increase in job loss. After the World War II industrial nations had economic growth worldwide that brought social stability, but the oil crisis in 1973 brought the advanced industrial nations including the USA enormous economic pressure.

Psychological Impact

The USA was proud that they had enough amounts of underground resources for the next ten years. During the oil crisis, however, people were shocked to the fact that they could not go without the Middle Eastern oil. They learned a lesson that it was not possible to be a powerful nation without oil, during waiting for hours in front of gas stations to buy 5 gallons of gas. They had lived with a lifestyle that consumption is like loving their nation, but now they realized the importance of prudence. President Nixon had his cabinet meeting in November to consider counterplans. On November 7th, Nixon issued a statement for people of saving energy, including suggestions like car-pool, lowering temperature of heating systems, night-lights only on top floors of multi-storied buildings, and turning off the neon-signs. Specially, he established a energy-development office to suggest self-supply without depending on foreign energy. That was, however impossible. The embargo of oil-export to the USA brought a lack of oil, confusion, distrust of oil companies, fear, and insecurity.

Disunion Among Allied Nations

The embargo on the oil export caused economic problems and economic problems brought political issues, and political issues resulted in world problems. The reason for that was the Arabian oil countries would not supply oil to the USA but also refused to supply oil to the US allied nations. Those countries had to choose to either have no oil supply by supporting the US or break allegiance ally with the US and get oil supplies.

In the meantime, Yamani and another minister of oil from Algeria visited European countries, threatening them not to supply oil if they agreed with the US policy that supported Israel. During the colonial period, the USA was always more generous than the European countries. If there were any problems between European countries and colonial countries, the USA usually helped colonial countries. As a result, France lost northern African oil countries such as Algeria and Libya, and the UK gave up the Iranian oil field. When they had Suez Canal crisis in 1967, the UK gave up Suez under the US pressure, and the two countries began disuniting politically. As I mentioned above, the ultimate purpose of European Community was to be independent from a showdown between the US and the Soviet Union. As a matter of a fact, the US was not totally dependent upon Arabian oil.

There are huge oil fields in the USA. After they found the third largest oil field of the world in Alaska in December 1967, they produced 300 million barrels of oil per day. European countries, however, totally depended on the Middle Eastern oil. During Suez Canal crisis, the US was able to supply oil to Europe, but now, the US oil tanks are almost empty.

Europe could not but solve the problem for themselves. After all, the EU oppose the US policy, and issued a statement in

November of that year that they supported the Arabs, not Israel. The Netherlands was the only country that supported the USA. Accordingly, the Arabs tried not to send one drop of oil to the Netherlands. Because of the purpose of EC to form a community market, however, the Netherlands was able to get oil from other regions than from Middle East.

Arabs threatened Japan in the same way ; if Japan supported the US, they would not sell oil to them. Japanese enterprises had been in a very prosperous condition after the war. When the oil crisis began in 1973, Japanese businessmen suggested to their government to change their Middle Eastern policy to continue to import oil, for they knew oil had a direct relation to the Japanese economy. Kissenger called the Japanese Minister of Foreign Affairs in to his office to ask for support as an allied nation. A few days later, however, Danaka, the Prime Minister of Japan, issued a statement that they would support the Arabs. It was an example, showing callousness international policy. The US was like a benefactor to Europe, and Japan was able to reconstruct the country with the US help after the war. In the middle of crisis, however, they all isolated the USA and walked away for their own benefits. The oil weapon brought disunity among the US allied nations, influencing on international policies.

The Future of Oil

Oil is not a factory-product. It will be ended when it is no longer in reserves. The Middle Eastern reserves will last only for 40 or 50 years. Of course reserves have been increased after they found oil fields in Alaska and the northern sea. Oil-need has been radically increased, because less developed countries try their best efforts to develop their industries and number of vehicles has been increased.

After the energy crisis in 1973, scientists have searched for alternative resources for energy, for example, solar energy, wind, or tide energy. It has not been found something as good, cheap, and safe as oil, yet. It is said that energy from a nuclear reactor would be the most possible alternative, though it is risky.

Death

The third weapon that Islam Revolution militant might uses would be death. In some translation of Bible, this word, Death translated as disease, or plague. In Greek it is THAVATOS, which means the infectious disease, contagious disease, an epidemic. It can be interpreted that Islam uses an epidemic to kill many. This is hard to infer. How do they produce an epidemic to kill human race?

Some scholars interpret this, explaining that there is close relationship between famine and an epidemic. Scientifically, however, it has not been proven that famine brings an epidemic. Upon a long time of study on this verse, I think it would be appropriate to interpret this verse with two aspects:physically and spiritually.

Physically, this epidemic can be possibly interpreted as a bacteriological weapon(Bio-Weapon). On February 2000, Nightline of ABC, one of the US TV networks, showed a week long series on "Biological War." What will happen and what counter plans we should prepare against it. It was shock to the viewers. On the last day of the series, several mayors of larger cities agreed that there was the possibility of a Bio-War and discussed the counter plans.

One of the scenarios went like this:a guerrilla from a hostile country threw a bottle of a bacterial weapon into a subway station. Tens of thousands of wounded people, who were on their way home after work, were rushed to hospitals. There were not enough beds in any hospitals, and lacked antibiotic. Tens of thousands of people died in one day due to the lack of antibiotics. The next day, a transporting plane from the army delivered antibiotics, but it was too late. The entire city was ruined.

The most terrifying weapons in modern war are nuclear weapons, chemical weapons, and bacterial warfare weapons. To produce nuclear weapon it takes enormous time, skills, and expenses. Bacterial weapon, however, are simpler to make. Gather bacteria from infectious cases of epidemic and grow them. If Islamic countries fight with western European countries, it must be guerrilla warfare instead of a full-scale war. We have seen the two powers, the US and the Soviet Union, were defeated by guerilla warfare in Afghanistan and Vietnam even with modern scientific weapons. Islamic guerrilla had a winning experience in

Afghanistan. Bacterial weapons will not only bring about a massacre but also have a terrible psychological effect.

Spiritually, it infers that Islam will be spread all over the world like an epidemic, killing many souls.

Wild Beasts

The fourth weapon that Islam might use a wild beast. The literal interpretation of the phrase, "··· killed by wild beasts" is not appropriate. Which wild beast can kill so many people? If so, they will be shot. Therefore, wild beasts are symbolic expression. Wild beasts may be symbolized as human being(s) like wild beasts, those who are without reasoning and conscience.

Everyday, we read a newspaper reporting homicide(s). Several years ago in South Carolina a divorced young mother pushed her car with her two children in it into a lake to kill them because her new boy friend did not want to raise her children. Another wife killed her husband to receive her husband's life insurance money. A son killed his own parents to get his inheritance. Mass killings happened in the name of a religious sect. In Rwanda, fifty thousand women and children were killed after tribal fights. In Yugoslavia, women were raped in a tribal war. After energy crisis of 1973, the most horrible and hostile incidents have happened all over the world. In Japan, people from one of the religious sects named "Ouum" put toxic gas in a subway in Tokyo, killing many people. Analyzing these terrible incidents draws a conclusion that human beings have become like wild beasts without reason and conscience. Philosophers call this age "the age of the loss of humanity", that is, an age of human-animal.

Today, the problems of humankind that we face are serious. Science and technology have been advanced while morality and ethic have been withdrawn. It can be illustrated by a bird, which has one short wing and another long, is constantly falling down, losing a balance. There was a German philosopher who praised the German people as the best people in the world. How would he say this after Hitler brutally killed 6 million Jews during the World War Ⅱ? Consider those incidents that Japanese militarists usurped Korea and China, killing and savagery, that massacres and purging acts by communists in Russia and Korea, and that racial cleaning happened recently in Yugoslavia and Africa. We are living in an age of our losing humanity.

It is easily understood the phrase "killed by wild beasts" by recalling how cruel Islamic guerrilla were. International law implies that foreign embassy belong to the specific country. Who, however, threatened and abducted one of the staffs of the US embassy at Teheran for 444 days? Who bombed the Pam Am flight 103, which was flying across the Atlantic Ocean and killed innocent people on a Christmas vacation? Who bombed the 110-story Trade Center building in New York? Who bombed the US embassy in Kenya and in other countries?

George Otis wrote in his book, "The Last Enemy" about unbelievable facts of Islamic suicide unit at the war against Iraq:

Homeini often said about the paradise and the martyr. He recruited young boys – even some were less than 10 years old-for suicidal mission···. Homeini said, "Our people do not want to submit to humiliation and meanness any more. We want a bloody death rather than humiliating life. We are ready to be killed, and have made a covenant with our God to follow Hussein, who is our leader and lord of martyrs" ··· Then the boys left a piece of note ··· They were sent to the battlefield to clean minefields with their own feet. In their note, it was written, "Battlefield is my wedding and martyr is my bride. When preaching begins with the sound of firing, I will put on bloody wedding clothes. My bride of martyr will bear a son of freedom. I will leave my son, freedom, with you. Please take good care of him."

We know that this Islamic suicide unit bombed the US Embassy and the US Marine Corps barracks in Beirut. This cruel Islamic suicide unit can be interpreted as the wild beast. Islam has concentrated all energies to make the whole world Islamic world with those four kinds of weapons. It might be true when Huntington said that though the recent battles against Islam were not full-scale wars but they were quasi- wars. They might attack to major cities of US, some day, if we do not wake us up.

A Summary of four horses

From Chapter 7 to 10, I mentioned about four horses which are the four wars in the last days. I will summarize them:

1. White Horse(Rev. 6:1-2) The Colonial War

It was the Western Colonial War. It was the providence of God that the Gospel have been spread out to all of the world trough the waves of the Western colonialism, to fulfill the prophecy of Matt. 24:14.

2. Red Horse(Rev. 6:3-4) The Ideological War

It was the Communist Revolutionary War, so called the Ideological War or Cold War.

It was the providence of God to fulfill the prophecy of Luke 21:29-31. The fig tree and all the trees would sprout leaves.

3. Black Horse(Rev. 6:5-6) The Economic War

The Economic War was started by the European Union Movement. The Cold War was ended and the communist nations have been collapsed, and opening the door for the Gospel to communist world and the small and weak races under the communist power have been independent.

4. Pale Horse(Rev. 6:7-8) The Islam Revolutionary War

This war will make a serious problem of the would economy and the cause of the World War III. Revelation 9:14-16:

"Then the six angels blew his trumpet, I heard a voice coming from the four corners of the gold alter standing before God, The voice said to the six angels－release the four angels who are bound at the Euphrates River! The four angles were released:for this very hour of this very day, of this very month and year, they had been kept ready to kill a third of all the human race, I was told the number of the mounted troops；it was hundred million"

The world War III would be the last war in the history of the world, we call it as The Euphrates War, The Armageddon War, or the Last War.

Chapter 11
The Fifth Seal(Martyrs' Prayers)

"When he opens the fifth seal, I saw under the altar the souls of those who had been slain because of the word of God and the testimony they had maintained. They called out in a loud voice, "How long, Sovereign Lord, holy and true, until you judge the inhabitants of the earth and avenge our blood?" Then each of them was given a white robe, and they were told to wait a little longer, until the number of their fellow servants and brothers who were to be killed as they had been was completed"(Rev. 6:9-11, NIV).

When he opens the fifth seal, there appear no more horses but martyrs who appeal to God for judgment. They must ask God to judge the evil and to restore the kingdom of God on behalf of the saints who have been persecuted and tortured in the world. They, however, are told that persecution and sufferings would be continued until the number of martyrs will be completed.

Would this tribulation happen before the second coming? Or

after the second coming, that is, the seven-year Great Tribulation? Or is it introduction to the Great Tribulation?

I think this would not be the Great Tribulation, but indicate those who died under worldwide persecutions at the end of the world before the Lord's second coming.

The seven-year Great Tribulation will start with sounding the seven trumpets and the seven bowls' calamity. The seven trumpets have not been sounded yet. Therefore, it is foretold that there would be worldwide persecutions in the period between opening the first seal and the second coming.

When the world Protestant missionary movement started in the early eighteenth century, numerous missionaries were sent from Great Britain, the USA, and other European countries. There were few countries that welcomed the missionaries who brought the Gospel. Accordingly, wherever they went the missionaries and the first believers were killed under severe persecutions, trials, and tribulations.

That was the same in the early church history of Korea. We know the significant history of Roman Catholic Church. In 1846, the first Korean Father, Dae Kun Kim, martyred at the age of 25, about one year after he was ordained. After that persecution continued. In his book, "Korean Church History", Dr. Allen D. Clark describes:

In 1846, the first Korean Father, Dae Kun Kim got arrested, and there arose another severe persecution at the same time. It lasted for a long time. Persecution seemed never ceasing, and they continually killed the believers. Dae Won Kun was against foreign powers and against Christ. In 1866, there was a great persecution. He arrested many Christians from all the places. He captured ten French missionaries and killed them at Sae Dang Tuh. They continued to capture thousands of believers, and to kill hundreds of Christians in that place. They killed those who had the Bibles and who were believers, and they got rid of the Christian books. About two thousand people had been killed until the year of 1868(Korean translation, pp. 6-9).

Reading this, we know how severe persecutions were in the early Roman Catholic history.

The persecution history of the Protestant church was well known, too. The first Protestant martyr was the missionary Robert Jermain Thomas. He shed his blood at the Dae Dong River. The blood of the early Christian martyrs overflowed in the Korean peninsula because of misunderstanding, the persecutions under Japanese imperialism, persecutions toward North Korean Church by the communist party after liberation, and of the brutal killings by communists during the Korean War.

Those persecutions and tribulations toward Christian missionaries and early Christians happened not only in Korea, but also in Japan, China, India, or any place in the world. Especially, when the Communist Revolution began in the early nineteenth century communists declared religion as opium, and targeted the Church for revolution, and persecuted the Church most severely since the days of Roman persecution. In his research, "From 1900 until 1975", Ralph Winter, a professor of Fuller Theological Seminary, estimated that the Christian martyrs from the first century to 1900 were about 5,000,000, but those from 1900 to 1975 were at least 25,000,000.

Today, martyrs' blood is still flowing somewhere in the world. A Korean medical missionary couple was killed in Russia after the Cold War. In Nigeria, the Muslims recently killed the Christians and burned their churches. In Rwanda, it was recently reported that sixteen Catholic priests and many Christians were killed. Sufferings and persecutions will be continued until the numbers of martyrs would be completed.

There are some issues that we should speculate in the fifth seal.

The believers would not be persecuted but be lifted up

I heard preachers' preaching from my youth not to worry about persecutions, for the believers would not get any. They insisted that how would the good God let his children go through such severe persecutions. I agreed with them, too. However, when communism invaded North Korea and started to oppress the Christians I also got arrested and put in the jail for three days, tortured without food. Numerous believers shed their blood in North Korea under the Communist Party.

Teaching that the believers would not be persecuted before the Second Coming can possibly make the believers not to prepare for the coming persecutions and make them weaker in their faith.

The problem of faith of the martyrs' offspring

America is the country where the children of the martyrs first came by the Mayflower to keep their faith. They were called the Puritans. Significant persons such as John Knox and their fathers shed their blood to keep their faith and established Protestant churches in Europe. Because of their ancestors' faith, God has blessed America to become the world's most powerful country within two hundred years.

Today, however, a martyr's faith is hardly found in America. They seem to worship money and pleasure as their gods. Until the early 1970s, America was the country of Puritans. They had to go buy groceries and gas before 5 o'clock on Saturday afternoon because the shops were closed on Sundays. From 1970s, they began to open their shops on Sunday, showing their desire for making money instead of honoring God. Because of their depraved faith, God began to punish America. They were engaged in a war with Vietcong, spending $150,000,000,000. In 1975, however, they lost the war, giving Vietnam to the communist Vietcong. It was a shameful loss in American history. In 1973, economic crisis began and the government owed about $5,000,000,000,000. Moreover, it has been serious problems in moral corruptions, such as drugs, homicide, juvenile delinquencies, increasing divorce rate, pornography, etc. Who could say that this country is the descendents of the Puritans?

Emphasis on the martyrs' faith

The Lord said, "When the Son of Man comes, will he find faith on the earth?"(Luke 18:8). We should learn the martyrs' faith so that we could win the victories over any persecutions and sufferings. One of the important roles of the contemporary church is to make disciples and train them according to the mindset of the martyrs. However, many churches today are likely to incline to 'health and wealth gospel' or materialism. The glory of martyrdom is the supreme glory in the kingdom, and if the church does not produce believers who participate this supreme glory it will be blamed.

Sufferings that we bear today for the sake of the Lord cannot be compared to the glories to come. Therefore, we should be armed with martyrs' faith and deny ourselves and obey Him.

In American history, Christians have not been persecuted because of their faith yet. There have been, however, different kinds of enemies from whom many Christians have been persecuted and suffered. They are so called materialism, pleasures, peace-at-any-price, free-sex, drugs, homosexuality, corruption, and so forth. American Christians, however, fear persecutions, so they tend not to resist these enemies. They try to compromise with enemies and to justify them. They are like the priests and Levites on the way to Jericho who pass by and ignore those enemies ; even America has become a place like Sodom and Gomorrah. Of course it is not as easy to fight against them as against persecutions from communism or totalitarianism to maintain the faith. We are, however, soldiers of Christ and descendants of Martin Luther. Why are we not courageous and strong? If the churches and Christians in America would change their lives under the power of the Holy Spirit and begin a new life with martyrs' spirit, then it will become a new nation before long.

Chapter 12
Opening the Sixth Seal
(Historical Judgment)

"I watched as he opened the sixth seal. There was a great earthquake. The sun turned black like sackcloth made of goat hair, the whole moon turned blood red, and the stars in the sky fell to earth, as late figs drop from a fig tree when shaken by a strong wind. The sky receded like a scroll, rolling up, and every mountain and island was removed from its place. Then the kings of the earth, the princes, the generals, the rich, the mighty, and every slave and every free man hid in caves and among the rocks of the mountains. They called to the mountains and the rocks, 'Fall on us and hide us from the face of him who sits on the throne and from their wrath of the Lamb. For the great day of their wrath has come, and who can stand?'"(Revelation 6:12-17, NIV)

This is a clear picture of God's judgment. The issue is how to interpret this passage. As symbolic, literal, historical, or final judgment. If we interpret them literally, it will be very complicated to interpret the following verses that "after this⋯⋯" putting a seal on the forehead of 144,000 from the chapter 7 verse 1. Literally, it should be the final judgment, and after the final judgment there should be none left behind and nothing else could be happened in the world. However, in 7:1 it is written to put a seal on foreheads starting with "after this." Therefore, this passage should be interpreted as symbolic.

There are three kinds of judgment:

1. Conscientious judgment
2. Historical judgment
3. Final judgment

Conscientious judgment deals with lies to justify one's fault. It is accused by one's own conscience. Pilate sentenced Jesus death without finding any sin. It has been told that he had insomnia from his conscientious suffering and nightmares of trying to wash blood of his own hands. With any excuses, conscience knows the truth and accuses guilt.

The final judgment brings the end of the human history by God.

Historical judgment is the reign of God over human history with his justice and righteousness. In human perspective, it deals with reaping what you plant. Each individual, family, or nation will reap what he or she planted. God rules over an individual, family, peoples, and nation with justice. If I make another afflicted, I will be afflicted, too. Betrayal with betrayal, deception with deception.

The reason for this principle is to give us chances to repent. It shows his mercy. According to the passage, any worldly powers such as kings, princes, the general, the rich, or the mighty cannot escape from God's judgment.

If so, what kind of historical events were inferred in this passage? I view this as both World War I and II. Those were God's judgment on human history, especially toward those who were against Christianity. If Germany, Italy, and Japan won the war, Christianity would be enormously persecuted by them and Christianity could be used just as political affairs.

I visited Japan in 1965 for the first time. The Asian Christian Laymen Conference was held in Tokyo, and I was invited as one of the speakers. After the conference we took a trip to Hiroshima. A young minister, Danaka, guided me so I asked him to show me the place where the bomb was dropped. I had two reasons:first, I wanted to know how powerful it was that Japan surrendered and second, I wanted to see God's historical judgment on Japan which committed brutal barbarities toward the Korean people. I had hatred toward the Japanese from my youth. Because my grandfather joined the independent movement against Japanese imperialism, the Japanese military policemen invaded my home and arrested my grandfather. We did not understand what was happening, but we cried out to them not to take him. They kicked us, and we were terrified with fear.

The Japanese forced us to worship their idols, and took away the church bells. They put all the members of Je Am Ree Church into the church and burned them alive on Sunday. How many patriots were killed by the Japanese? I remember following Danaka's guide on that day, thinking, "What kind of judgment did God bring to the brutal Japan?" Danaka must not know what was in my mind on that day. He guided me to a museum at the Peace Park, where they exhibit the pictures of the city at that time. On the first wall, they put the pictures of the city Hiroshima before bombing, and it looked as large as Seoul. On the second wall, there were the pictures of the B 29, from which dropped the bomb, and the two bottle-sized bombs that were dropped to Hiroshima and Nagasaki. On the third wall, the picture of bombing like a huge mushroom, and on the fourth wall the pictures of the ruins. Everything was destroyed but several chimneys. On the next wall, they put three major newspapers such as Asahi, Yomiuri, and Mainizzi that reported the bombing with big pictures. I can't forget one of their headlines saying, "The river was not flowing because of the human bodies." The bombing killed people but more people were dead because of radioactive contaminated water.

I visited the hospital on the hill where the wounded people were in. They flew the American flag and Japanese flag together. The place made me imagine hell. I was not able to make any eye contact with those who were deformed as the result from fire. I was trying to say something to one of the women, but surprisingly, she was a Christian. She said to me, weeping, "Sir, God punished Japan because of the sins against Korea." God's judgment toward human history is serious and fearful. The judgment of this passage and the Hiroshima bombing seem alike each other.

The prophesy of the fifth seal is about the salvation history from 1800 till now. Most martyrs were killed during this period in history of Christianity. The sixth seal is prophesying the world history. It is about God's judgment on human history, especially on anti-Christian countries. God will continue to control and judge human history until the Second Coming.

Chapter 13

The Opening of the Seventh Seal

(After the Cold War and the Middle East Conflicts)

"When he opened the seventh seal, there was silence in heaven for about half an hour. And I saw the seven angels who stand before God, and to them were given trumpets"(Rev. 8:1-2, NIV).

"Silence" stands for a period of peace, without war, that is, secession of the Cold War tensions. "Half an hour" means for while, literally 30 minutes. "Trumpet" denotes impending war. A trumpet is necessary device in war ; they are assigned for an advance, a rush, a retreat, a rest, or a meal.

Fear of the Cold War

"Silence in the heaven" foretold the coming of the secession of the Cold War. We have already discussed the sixth seal as God's judgment on human history. After the World War II, the USSR communists were trying to have a world revolution against western democracy, so the two powers started having conflicts.

The USSR offered weapons and bullets with their ideology to other countries, and made every effort to try to overrun their governments in order to expand its influence toward the whole world. They were successful to overturn China, which has one fourth of the world population, turning it into a communist country. They also manipulated the Korean War, and continued to fire up Vietnam, Laos, Cambodia, and the Japanese Red Army, Angola Civil War, Central and South American guerrillas, and the Black War that Arab attacked Israel in 1973. The Cuban crisis and the Middle East conflict in 1973 almost drove us into the World War III, which has not been happened. The period of Cold War was an era of fear and anxiety. Nobody guessed when the third world war would burst out. There were about 1,700,000,000 people starving to death, yet the world consumed money to compete the war expenditure. Both the USA and the USSR were armed with guided missiles and multi-warhead missiles, consequently, everybody was terrified with the possibility of a nuclear war. The era of the Cold War was that of fear and attrition.

Coming of the Secession of the Cold War

It is written in the book of Revelation 7:1, "After this I saw four angels standing at the four corners of the earth, holding back the four winds of the earth to prevent any wind from blowing on the land or on the sea or on any tree." This prophesies how the era of the secession of the Cold War coming. That is, four angels held the wind, and there was peace without wind in the earth. It is reasonable to view the wind as World War III, and the four angels as four powers who opened an era of peace.

Looking back over the history of the early 1970s, the two giants, the USA and the USSR took control over the world. However from the mid 1970s, China separated from the USSR, and the European countries had stood as independent powers. Now the world has become four powers. This might be interpreted as the four angels. I would like to discuss the reason why the four powers have come.

The separation between the USSR and China

They issued "a Moscow Manifesto" at the Delegation Conference of Communist Parties from 81 countries on December 6, 1960. The Chinese communist party, however, criticized severely the USSR as "contemporary modifier", for its peaceful coexistence with the USA. Then the USSR canceled the treaty with China for economic and technological assistance, and they withdrew all the workers from China. It impacted Chinese economy a great deal. In 1962, the conflict became worse because of Cuban crisis, China-India boundary dispute, and partial banning of the nuclear test. The USSR summoned its army from Europe, and replaced them at the border of China. China-USSR problem became serious when they had armed conflicts on the border in March, July, and August in 1969. China remembered the USSR's invasion into

Czechoslovakia, and feared they might try and do the same to them. At that time, president Nixon was concerned about this possible critical situation, that the USSR could eat up China, which would make things worst for the USA, so it retested it's Chinese policy. Kissinger, the Secretary of the State, secretly went to Beijing through Pakistan, and prepared a way for Nixon to visit Beijing to settle down their relationship.

Nixon and Mao Tse-tung issued a "Shanghai Joint Declaration" on February 21, 1972 in Beijing, and the Republic of China was officially recognized as the representative of whole China, and became a member of the Security Council of the United Nations. Nixon and Kissenger had changed their blockade policy from a showdown to negotiation.

Nixon visited Moscow in May 1972, and had a summit conference with Brezhnev. Brezhnev was afraid that China might become a strong nation, so he tried to convince Nixon to control China by "we, whites" or "we, Europeans." Nixon made good use of the "China card" to negotiate with USSR. Consequently, the Strategic Arms Limitation Talks(SALT) was issued. Of course, China used the USA card to resolve the boundary conflict and others, too.

European Independence

European countries had formed a community and gradually separated from influences of the USA. They formed Economic Community, and in January 1999 they began to use unified money. In the fall of the same year they integrated the Joint Headquarters displaying their political, economical, militarily independent power.

In 1980, President Carter appealed to entire Europe to boycott the Moscow Olympics because of Afghanistan invasion. Only West Germany responded to that appeal, but almost all the other European countries participated in the Olympics. President Reagan tried to stop connecting gas pipes from the USSR to Europe, but he was not successful either. Europe has become completely independent power.

As the USSR knew it was impossible to win a war against the USA without Chinese cooperation, so did the USA without European cooperation. By the early 1970s, the capacity of the nuclear weapon possessed by both countries was TNT 15 ton for each individual in the world. If they were used the human history would be end. As the world began its history of the four powers, so the secession of the Cold War has opened. One passage of Revelation was fulfilled.

INF Agreement

In December 1987, Brezhnev visited the USA, discussing the reduction of armaments with President Reagan and they signed an INF(Intermediate-range Nuclear Force) Treaty. Thus, the era of secession of the Cold War has begun. This treaty was the largest amount of reduction ; they agreed to withdraw and disarm all the short-range ballistic missiles and mid-range ballistic missiles from Europe and Asia. They decided to co-supervise the process by both generals. By this treaty, both USA and the USSR agreed to avoid war and consequently, the USSR began to open its door to the world.

After the USSR open-door principle, the eastern European countries were freed from its strong influence and began to be independent and to join the United Nation. Spring came upon the Iron Curtain. The Russian people also had freedom, at the same time the underground churches began to be identified. Missionaries from all over the world come and preach freely the Gospel. Nobody foretold that the headquarters of communist revolution would be fallen like that. The prophecy has been fulfilled when the time, when the Lord, the king of all kings who reigns over human history has come.

God's Will For the Era
of Secession of the Cold War

There are two purposes for the Lord's will toward the era of the secession of the Cold War. They have already been fulfilled.

The Fulfillment of Luke 21:29-31

"He told them this parable:Look at the fig tree and all the trees. When they sprout leaves, you can see for yourselves and know that summer is near. Even so, when you see things happening, you know that the kingdom of God is near."

The fig tree's sprouting leaves is the prophesy of Israel's independence, and it was fulfilled on May 14, 1948. Many historians were negative about Israel's independence. They said it would be impossible for a country to get independence after 400 years being a colony, for they had been identified with the ruling country. That had not been the case, either. However, the word of God is always true, so it came true beyond the historical cases.

The generation before us died without seeing the day of Israel's independence. When I was young my grandfather took me to a revival tent meeting for the first time. They had drums and clapped their hands, which was very new to me, singing hymns. The speaker's name was Nam Soo Chung. I still remember the lyrics and melody:

Oh how blessed / The glorious hope / I will be transformed on the day /
When Jesus comes again
The fire flames / That I have hoped for / Waiting and waiting / For the Lord comes again

Israel is restored / for the glory of Jerusalem / Amen, Lord Jesus, Amen / Come now quickly

It was 1936, when I was eight years old. I still hear his passionate message:

"Every nation in the world set policies for its own benefit, and for the sake of the nation's benefit, it is willing to have a war. Therefore, they speak about peace, but peaceful world will never come. Only when Jesus comes again, who died for the world, and rules over the world, and then there will be a real peace in the world. That is why the Lord comes again. The Lord said that he would come when Israel gets independence. Israel will be independent before long. We should pray for Israel's independence."

The saints who died before May 15, 1948 did not see the word fulfilled, though they might anticipate it. Those who died before 1989 did not see the fulfillment of Jesus' prophesy, "All the trees sprout leaves." We, however, have witnessed with our eyes for the past 10 years that Luke 21:29 was fulfilled. These prophecies are the "wake up call" for today's church from the Lord. Those who have ears listen to the word of God.

Fulfillment of Matthew 24:14
"And this Gospel of kingdom will be preached in the whole world as a testimony to all nations, and then the end will come."

The prophecy on the Christianity becoming the most prevailing religion in the world seems almost impossible. Jesus told this prophecy right before he was caught on the Mount Olive. His disciples were unlearned and cowardly men, so they all fled away when Jesus got caught. It was hardly imagined that those people would preach the Gospel with boldness.

They, however, were filled with the Holy Spirit on the day of

Pentecost and began to preach at the cost of their lives. The Roman persecution toward the Early Church was too harsh to describe. Early Christians did not give up, and won the Roman power. As a result, Gospel was preached to all over Europe. The world mission movement arose in England in the eighteenth century fired up the vision for evangelizing the entire world. It became declined, however, when the Russian Communist movement started in the early nineteenth century. Communists persecuted the church, imprisoned and killed ministers, and closed churches.

That lasted for about seventy-five years and it seemed impossible to evangelize the world and to be fulfilled Jesus' prophecy. After the Cold War, however, the USSR opened a door for the Gospel. Missionaries from all over the world do their jobs ; there are about 650 missionaries sent by Korea, preaching the Gospel.

I visited Moscow in October 1994 for the first time. A missionary, whom our church had supported, invited me. The purpose of that trip was to do mission. It was right after Russia opened its door, and it seemed chaotic ; poor public security, economic depression due to inflation, and not enough food. To me, the Russian Communist revolution, which was to make the world a paradise, seemed declining with poverty and evil spirit.

We planned, and I led an evangelical conference at downtown of Moscow. I spoke English, and a translator translated into Russian. From the first day, the auditorium was full of people who were hungry for the word of God, and every night hundreds of people came to the altar to receive Jesus Christ, their Savior and Lord. It was the most exiting moment in my life. I thought, 'I am preaching the word of God at the Headquarter of the world communists ···' I remember that day when I preached to the cadets at the Military Academy. Hundreds of cadets raised their hands to receive Jesus Christ and I thought I was dreaming.

These surprising events have happened for the last ten years. This is the last chance that God has opened doors for his missions. He has given the era of secession of the Cold War to preach the Gospel to the end of the world. It is our mission.

But It Is Only For 30 Minutes

"There was silence in heaven for about half an hour."

It is time for us to awake to accomplish our mission. It will last only for 30 minutes. How long will it be God's time for half an hour into human time? It should not be long. If we do not accomplish the mission, living and loving the world and ignoring God's warning, then we would be like the "five virgins" and the servant who got one talent.

Chapter 14
The Last War of Human History

"And I saw the seven angels who stand before God, and to them were given seven trumpets."

The age of "silence in heaven for about half an hour", that is, the era of the secession of the Cold War, the seven angels are given seven trumpets from God. In chapters 8 and 9, they blew the trumpets ; it is time to burst out the last war in human history. This is called the Middle East War or Armageddon. It is the last war written in the book of Revelation, and it is prophesied that one third of world population will die in this war.

I found it very difficult to interpret this war. I have researched and studied on this issue for a long time, and I finally figured out the answer. The problems related to this issue are found in 9:14-16.

1. It is prophesied that this war would burst out in the Euphrates

River, which is a dessert area, not a military fortress. Why would it be this place?

2. It is written that the four angels were bound. What are the four angels?

3. The number of mounted troops was two hundred million. Who are they? And which nations would participate in this war?

4. One third of mankind will be killed in this war. What kind of weapon would be used to kill that many people?

5. This war would burst out at the Euphrates River(Iraq), but why will the middle of Israel, Armageddon, be the battle place?

The Beginning of the Last War

"And I saw the seven angels who stand before God, and to them were given seven trumpets."

It is written that it would come, the secession of the Cold War, and during that period the seven angels would be given trumpets. Trumpets infer war, the last war on earth. This war burst out at the Euphrates River(Rev. 9:14), that is, today's Iraq, where the River crosses over its land. Therefore, to fulfill this prophecy there should be a serious problem in Iraq in order to fire the flame of the last war. It was the Gulf War.

After the USA and the USSR jointed the INF treaty in June

1988, the era of the secession of the Cold War came. The world took an optimistic view that there would be no war for a while. However, in August 1990, Saddam Hussein of Iraq invaded Kuwait with 140,000 military armies and 1,800 tanks. Iraq occupied Kuwait so quickly that it completely surprised the whole world after the secession of the Cold War.

The reason for this invasion was that Saddam Hussein had no way to repay the loan borrowed from Kuwait during the war against Iran. Hussein made up an excuse that Kuwait used to belong to Iraq and invaded it in the name of Arabic One Nation. Of course he had complained that Kuwait caused the oil price to go down by producing more than the quota measured by the OPEC. His true intention was to occupy Kuwait and Saudi Arabia with military force in order to control 40 percent of the world oil products and to rule over the world through Arabic oil weapon. He made a wrong estimation that time just as he did against Iran.

It is considered that the America's policy toward Iraq contributed to Hussein's miscalculation. Bush's administration loaned 550,000,000 to Iraq, selling weapons to support Iran-Iraq war. They had close relationship, and even planned for joint military training in July 1990. The USA friendly policy toward Iraq should have reviewed in advance and been based on principles.

Right after Iraq's invasion President Bush appealed to the world leaders to criticize and punish Iraq. The next day, Baker, the Secretary of the State, issued a joint declaration in Moscow with Saber de Naze, the Minister of the Foreign Affairs of the USSR, in order to force the world not to sell weapons to Iraq. On August 2, the UN Security Council took an oath to compulsory arbitration if Iraqi military would not withdraw from Kuwait. Four days later the economic sanction to ban import oil from Iraq and Kuwait became effective.

On August 6, Baker and Cheney(Dick Cheney, the Minister of National Defense) visited Saudi Arabia, finding out that Saudi had been threatened by Iraq, so they agreed to place US military in Saudi Arabia. From the next day, they started to send 200,000 airborne corps an armed division, and fighters to Saudi Arabia. Other western countries, Egypt, Morocco, and Syria also sent militaries. Of course the United Nation supported this plan.

On August 8, President Bush announced to chastise the invader if Hussein would not accept the following items:

1. Iraqi military should withdraw immediately from Kuwait without condition.
2. The legal government of Kuwait should be returned as soon as possible.
3. The USA is responsible for security and peace in Persian Gulf.
4. The Americans abroad should be protected.

However, Hussein, in spite of enormous pressure under the USA and the UN, dare to declare that they would use thousands of American and western hostages as human shields against the US offense. In early December, the number of US military army was increased up to 550,000, and multinational army was about 70,000. The United Nation Security Council warned Iraq they would be offended if it would not withdraw its military from Kuwait until January 15, 1991. Hussein rejected to withdraw unless Israel gave up Palestine.

President Bush asked the Congress to use military force and got permission. On January 16, 1991, they made an air raid on Iraq and Kuwait. On February 23 a ground army directed under general Schwartzkov marched toward Kuwait and Iraq, but Iraq was not able to resist. The road toward Basra, where the Iraqi withdrew from Kuwait, became like offences. Finally, Iraq accepted the twelve items imposed by the United Nation, and the war was concluded after 100 hours battle. President Bush declared that Iraq had lost the war and Kuwait had been set free, so the war ended.

From the Gulf war I learned the answers of the five questions mentioned above.

1) The reason for the prophecy written in Revelation that the final Middle East War would be burst out in Iraq though it is located in the dessert is because of oil. If it happens at oil fields, any country of the world could not help but become involved in wars. It is certain that the coming final Middle East War should become the world war because of oil. Experts estimate that the amount of oil reserves in Iraq would be the second of the world, after Saudi Arabia.

2) The reason why the four powers clash one another at the Euphrates River was understood from the lesson of the Gulf

War. It is now an era of the four super powers such as the USA, European Community, China, and Russia. The United States produces half of its demand. However, if it would be impossible to import oil because of war, its economy would fall into a great depression. Though Europe holds a little oil reserve in North Sea, its economy would fall quickly without importing oil from Middle East. China also needs to import oil from Middle East. Because of this need, China maintains friendly relationships with oil producing countries and supports militarily, providing weapons. Japan seems safe from Middle East because it is remote, but it bore one fifth of total war expenses, $110,000,000 of the Gulf War. It is certain that nobody in the world is safe when they have war at oil fields.

3) The Gulf War broke out while they were celebrating the era of the secession of the Cold War gives us an important lesson. Many experts foresaw that there would not be a full-scale war during that time. For example, a new expert of the National Safety of the USA, Michael O'Hanton, had an interview with a journalist in Korea(Yong Jung Chu, Chosun Daily News) in early 2000, and he said, "The probability of a war engaging the USA, Russia, or China will be lessened in the near future." However, even international political scientists or bright politicians seem not able to predict the future very well. If the USA would know in advance Iraqi invasion against Kuwait, it would not support Iraq-Iran war.

If the USA presumed Homaini would cause Islamic revolution, it would not help and support Sha, the king of Iran. Furthermore, it could avoid the historical contempt that the US embassy officers were incarcerated for 444 days. Many experts foresee that there would not be a full-scale war, but the book of Revelation says that there will be.

4) It has been answered the question why it is written in Revelation(16:16) that the final war field will be at central Israel, Armageddon. The USA was afraid that if the Gulf War would be expanded to the Islamic holy war. Therefore, President Bush asked Israel not to involve in the war, so it did. Saddam Hussein, however, offended Israel several times with scud missile. It is certain that if the Middle East War broke out, Israel would be the target no matter what. Therefore, it is clearly understood in the prophecy that the Middle East War should start in the Euphrates River, and will be spread to Armageddon.

5) At the final war in the world will involve 200,000,000 militaries, and one third of world population will be killed. From the Gulf War, this prophecy(Rev. 9:14-16) is also understood. 200,000,000 military soldiers infer that it will be a worldwide full-scale war, involving China and India. If a fire flames out in the oil field, every nation in the world will participate the war. In his book, "Civilization Clash", Huntington insists that China will take the central role in this war. He describes following scenarios on the war:

China will rise as a supreme country in the world in the early twentieth century. In 2010, the us military will be withdrawn from the reunited Korea. Taiwan will admit China as the suzerain state and its independence, and join the United Nation.

China will initiate southern China oil production, but the USA companies will take control of Vietnam Sea area.

China declares its lordship before whole areas in south Chinese Sea. As a result, China and Vietnam will have a naval battle. China will invade Vietnam to repay contempt held in 1979.

The USA will not overlook the Chinese invasion of Vietnam, and validate economic sanction. It will place an aircraft carrier at the South Chinese Sea, and start making air raids. The Secretary General of the United Nations and the Japanese Minister of Foreign Affairs try to suspend the hostilities, but will not be successful. Consequently, the war will be spread to East Asia.

Japan opposes the US offense against China, but the USA does not care. Japan declares its neutrality, and closes the US military base.

Chinese submarine and air force planes from China and Taiwan damage the US fleet. Chinese ground army marches on toward Hanoi, taking almost all of Vietnam.

The USA considers using nuclear weapons, but will be opposed by public opinion. Thus, it tries to end the war.

In the mean time, India attacks Pakistan in waves. Indian modern elite troops will be sent to Pakistan. Pakistan asks for Arabic countries to send military aid. India is conscious about Iran because of Southwest Asian countries.

Islam attacks Israel:Chinese winning over the USA encourages Islamic countries. Each pro-American Arabic country transfers in principles, and attacks Israel. It becomes impossible to check them in advance with the reduced Sixth Fleet.

Japan sympathizes with China, and joins the war with China. Japan seizes the US military bases in its land, so the US army will withdraw. The US military blocks the Japanese sea — the US and Japan have sporadic battles on the West Pacific. Japan becomes closer to China because of oil transport.

China will seize power all over East Asia and Russia will panic. Russia joins anti-China Allies and Associated Armies, and sends its troops to Siberia. The Chinese in Siberia disrupt Russian tactics. China sends troops to protect its people, so the battle spreads out. The belligerent military nations absolute need for oil and its transport. The western countries gradually depend on oil from Russia, Caucasus, and Central Asia

The USA makes every effort to get full-support from European Community. China threatens with the use of nuclear weapons warning European countries not to involve. However, NATO and the USA notify China that they would attack and get rid of Chinese missile base.

In the mean time, Serbia attacks Bosnia, and Croatia joins, too. They get rid of Bosnia and finish ethnic cleansing. Algeria attacks Europe with nuclear weapon, and Europe avenges, and attacks targeting areas in North Africa.

Allied armies of the USA, India, Russia, and Europe wage a full-scale war against China, Japan, and Islam. There is possibility for the allied army to defeat China, who takes control over East Asia.

From this battle, we can anticipate one of three possible happenings: (1) the world could be destroyed under the nuclear weapon, (2)

suspend the war, or (3) Russian and western troops will come into the Tienanmen Square.

Samuel Huntington describes imaginary world full-scale war in this book. The readers may think that the above scenario is an absurdity, but there is a probability and reality in cause of a war. His convictions on probability and reality of a war are based on the following.

Islam and China fought together against Hitler. Now Pakistan, Iran, Iraq, Syria, Algeria, Libya, and others together incorporate with China in various ways, by making weapons of mass destruction. China provided 22 percent of weapons used in Iran-Iraq war in 1980. In 1989, China was the country that sold the most weapons to Iran, supported Iranian desires to possess nuclear capabilities. In January 1990, China signed a treaty that it would help and support scientific technology and military technology transport for 10 years. They made a Nuclear Aid Treaty in 1992. In March 1993, China agreed to construct 300-megaton nuclear reactor, and provided uranium concentration devices. Pakistan provided training for Iranian scientists. In November 1992, Pakistan, Iran, and China, agreed to cooperate in nuclear development. These three countries are now cooperating to produce weapons of mass destruction. China continued to make close diplomatic relationships with Arabic oil producing countries. These series of incidents have happened while we were celebrating the secession of the Cold War and dreaming of peace. We realize that the preparation of the

Armageddon war has been processed according to the prophecy in the Book of Revelation.

Huntington is not a mere political scholar or scientific fiction novelist. He is the Albert Wether head professor of Harvard University and Chairman of John Olin Strategy Research Center. He was once a presidential aid of President Carter's Diplomatic-Security. He is a well-known scholar in military-politics and comparative politics. We need to pay attention to the fact that his conviction is beginning to come into accord with the prophecy in Revelation.

Pay Attention to the Middle East

We have to pay close attention to the Middle East. Because the book of Revelation tells us that the last war will start at the Euphrates River(Rev. 9:14), and it is prophesied, "The sixth angel poured out his bowl on the great river Euphrates, and its water was dried up to prepare the way for the kings from the East"(Rev. 16:12). As it has been proved so far, history has proceeded just as it is written in the book of Revelation. It will be also fulfilled in the future because the One who controls the human history is Father God, the King of all kings.

Before I read Huntington's book I guessed that China would be involved in the war to fulfill the number of 200,000,000 soldiers. After reading it, I have a deep assurance that China will take a central role with Islamic countries in a large-scale war.

The Last War in the World,
Killing Two Billion People

What kind of weapon will they use to kill one third of whole population in the world? The answer is written in Revelation 8:10-11.

"The third angel sounded his trumpet, and a great star, blazing like a torch, fell from the sky on a third of the rivers and on the springs of water-the name of the star is Wormwood. A third of the waters turned bitter, and many people died from the waters that had become bitter."

In Chapter 8, verse 7, it is written about the ground battle of the last war that will take place. God showed John a scary scene that one third of whole world was burning. In verses 8-9, is written about a naval battle. Revelation was written in the first century A.D. It describes modern war, while it was written even before gunpowder was invented. One third of naval fleets were destroyed in the war.

In verses 10-11, an air battle of the last war is prophesied. "A star blazing like a torch" infers a missile. 95 A.D., when the book of Revelation was written, they had not invented gunpowder yet. They had battles with swords, spears, and bows and arrows at that time. However, God showed John clearly contemporary weapons. What kind of bomb is attached on the warhead of missile that the waters become bitter enough to kill many people when it is broken? They must be using nuclear warheads, with chemical warfare, and germ bombs. When a nuclear weapon is exploded, the water is polluted by radioactivity and kills people who drink from it. A germ bomb does the same thing that kills people with horrible diseases. Those mass killing weapons used in the last war will kill one third of whole population in the world.

When Will This War Break Out?

It is written in the book of Revelation concerning the "time." The time is secretly kept. We may ask two questions:(1) Will this war start with oil in the oil age? Or (2) after the oil age when an alternative is found?

If it happens in the oil age, those nations who do not have oil fields will suffer desperately economically. Therefore, the powers might compromise diplomatically with oil producing countries. However, if the processing research on helium energy or solar heat energy will be developed in near future and practically used, then the powers might let a war go in the Middle East. Because if it happened at the oil age it would be like cutting off their own feet it can, therefore, be inferred that a war cannot happen at that time.

I believe it will happen in the oil age, for there would be no other reason for one third of whole population, which would be killed in the Euphrates River to happen. It is a barren and dessert area with nothing there except oil. Neither is it as important as

Suez Canal, nor a strategic location or transportation place, nor is it a world economic place with diamonds or gold. If we do not need oil any more after developing alternative energies, why do we bother, battling in the dessert with that expensive cost? On the other hand, scientists are concerned that the need is increasing each year, and even they find new oil fields and increase amount of oil production, it is predicted that it will be depleted in about 40 years. If it is assumed that the war begins in the oil age, then the conclusion is for this generation to see the war.

The Result of the War(Great Tribulation)

It is certain that the war, killing one third of whole population, should use mass killing weapons including nuclear weapon. When nuclear war breaks out, a nuclear winter will follow. Nuclear clouds will cover up the sun for many years, and there will be no crops. Scientists predict that animal farming will be also impossible because of plagues and droughts. This is the time of seven-year tribulation when the seven angels pour out the bowl on the ground in Revelation chapter 16.

Regarding the time of Jesus' Second Coming, there are three views ; before tribulation, during the tribulation, and after tribulation. These three schools insist their views, quoting the Bible verses. I believe Jesus' Second Coming before the tribulation is biblical and reasonable. However, I want readers not to waste their time discussing this matter. If they believe Jesus' coming again during the tribulation, there is just three and half years' difference. If they believe Jesus' coming after tribulation, they have seven years' difference. It is not important which view one believes. The fact that his coming is impending and this is the most important thing to remember and we should commit ourselves to accomplish our calling.

"When these things begin to take place, stand up and lift up your heads, because your redemption is drawing near"(Luke 21:28).

Chapter 15
The Last Wake Up Call

"Therefore keep watch, because you do not know on what day your Lord will come"(Matthew 24:42).

"If he comes suddenly, do not let him find you sleeping. What I say to you, I say to you everyone:'Watch!'"(Mark 13:36-7).

"Be always on the watch, and pray that you may be able to escape all that is about to happen, and that you may be able to stand before the Son of Man"(Luke 21:36).

"Behold, I come like a thief! Blessed is he who stays awake and keeps his clothes with him, so that he may not go naked and be shamefully exposed"(Revelation 16:15).

It Is the Time to Awake from Sleep

The first thing that we must do in this age is to awaken our spirits. Those who are in sleep cannot do anything. Only those are awake accomplish their mission. What does it mean by spiritual awakening?

I have experienced several revivals in my spiritual journey. It is not easy to stay awakened spiritually all times. To stay awakened, we need to know ourselves whether we are in spiritual sleep or spiritual awake. How do we know that? I will summarize based on my own spiritual experiences.

When we are in spiritual sleep, we lose inner peace, joy and thanksgiving

If one's spirit is awakened, he/she is always in peace. Even in times of troubles and hardships like stormy weather, one's heart is filled with peace of the Lord. She or he sings songs of joy, and gives thanksgiving and praise to the Lord. When we are in spiritual sleep, however, our prayer time become shorter and shorter, we lose inner peace, joy, and thanksgiving. Instead, we have hatred, envy, jealousy, lewdness, pleasure seeking, and materialism.

When we are in spiritual sleep, our prayer time gets shorter, we lose power of prayer, and our prayers are not answered

When we are awake, we spend long time in prayer, desiring to know God. There are two kinds of prayer. One is "my" prayer, and the other is the prayer of the Holy Spirit(Ephesians 6:18). When we are awake spiritually, we pray through the Holy Spirit. We sometimes spend whole night or many hours talking to the Lord. From those hours we get inspired and strengthened. C. M. Miles who wrote the hymn, "I Come to the Garden Alone", must have prayed through the Holy Spirit.

I Come to Garden Alone

By C. M. Miles

I come to the garden alone
While the dew still on the roses
And the voice I hear, falling on my ear
The Son of God disclose

And he walks with me
And he talks with me
And he tells me I am his own
And the joy we share
As we tarry there
None other has ever know

He speaks and the sound of his voice
Is so sweat the bird's hush they're singing
And the melody that he gave to me
Within my heart is ringing

I'd stay in the garden with him
Though the night around me be falling
But he bids me go through the voice of woe
His voice to me is calling

When we are in spiritual sleep, we lose sense of thanksgiving for his grace

When we are awake, day-by-day, we give thanks to God for the salvation, that he bore the cross for us, and our hearts are full of love for him. It is our joy to take our cross and follow him daily. Our eyes, we have tears of gratitude.

Our eyes, however, dry up when we are in spiritual sleep. Drying up tears of gratitude means that our heart is not for love for the Lord. We love the world more than the Lord. Nothing can be replaced to the love of God, when we are awake:with all our hearts, we praise him with love:

> I'd rather have Jesus than silver and gold
> I'd rather be His than have riches untold
> I'd rather have Jesus than houses or lands
> I'd rather be led by His nail pierced hand

> Then to be a King of vast do main
> And behold on sin's dread away
> I'd rather have Jesus than anything
> This world affords today

> I'd rather have Jesus than men's applause
> I'd rather be faithful to His dear cause
> I'd rather have Jesus than Worldwide fame
> I'd rather be true to His holy name

When we are in spiritual sleep, we spend less time in reading

and meditating the word of God, and lose the sweetness of the
word

We spend hours reading and meditating the word, love the word, and try to put them into practice daily. When I ministered to the local churches I did not need extra time to prepare sermons. I share with people my testimonies while I learned and experienced while I was reading and meditating the word daily, and people were usually experience the same grace. When I was in spiritual sleep, people did not receive what I preached, though I spent time preparing and studying for the sermons. I found out after many years' ministerial experiences that a sermon is not creating work but a testimony. The Holy Spirit works through the word. When the word is dried up, the work of the Holy Spirit is also. Rev. Sundu Kil, one of the early church leaders in Korea said, "To be filled with the Holy Spirit means to be filled with the word." Our spirit is in sleep when the word of God lacks.

We lose our passion for the souls while we are in sleep. When we are awake, whomever we meet, we check out whether he or she is saved or not. If one is unbeliever, we earnestly try to make him or her believer with passion. When we are in sleep, however, we do not care because we lose passion for the lost. If someone is drowning, we must jump into the water to save the one. We do not pass by like the Levite or the priest if a person is dying.

I have experienced that I became insensitive to the lost, not telling the Gospel to the unbelievers because I was in spiritual sleep. My conscience became dull. I preached people to tell the

Gospel to the world, but I myself did not do it at times. Paul said, "Woe to me if I do not preach the Gospel"(1 Corinthians 9:16). Like the first son in Luke 15, we sometimes misunderstand ourselves as good Christians because we come to church and worship God every Sunday. As the father's wish was to bring his second son back home, so God's wish is to bring the lost back to his home. Holiness without preaching, piety without preaching, orthodox without preaching, and worship without preaching are abomination before God.

What are the reason for some churches do not grow while others are growing?

Why one believer lead many people to the Lord while another bring no one to church? The answer is simple:sleeping churches or sleeping individuals do not preach the Gospel, and consequently, they cannot grow.

There are two big problems in modern churches. One is the act of false prophets under the influence of liberal theology that there are other ways to salvation except Jesus. The other is the problem of churches like Pharisees that they regard them as orthodox Christians, yet have no passion for evangelism and mission which is the focal point of the Biblical message and prior job for all Christians. In his book, "The Revival", Martin Lloyd Jones, a great preacher and writer who ministered to Westminster Church in London for about 25 years, calls churches that do not grow because of lack of passion for the souls "dead orthodox church."

***When we are in spiritual sleep, we lose wisdom and power
to overcome Satan and self***

When we are closer to God through the word, praise, and
prayers, we are able to overcome self and Satan with spiritual
power. Our faith journey is continuous fighting against self and
Satan. When we are awake, we have sense of the presence of
the Holy Spirit. Therefore, our spiritual eyes are open to see satanic
activities, leading us to a victory. We can win the victory in our
daily lives not with our own strength, but with his power.

Satan is jealous when we earnestly follow the Lord's Commission,
so it tries to distract us. Therefore, we must be always awake
spiritually not to be distracted by Satan. When I was spiritually
young, I spent long hours to defend myself against oppositions.
Later, I learned that it was foolish and childish. When he was
arrested and persecuted without any reason, Jesus did not defend
himself. He bore his cross silently, and he also tells us to follow
him. After I learned from Jesus, I have tried to follow him, bearing
my cross, not to fight against enemies but to concentrate on my
mission. As time passed, God dealt with my enemies. It is not
I who keep myself but the Lord, himself. He is sovereign over
every matter of life.

Satan tries every effort to knock me down. When I was successful
in something, Satan made me proud of myself through praises
and honors. When I was in spiritual sleep, I was not able to see

Satan's plots. I became proud, and fell. When I was awake spiritually, I gave praise to the Lord and glorify him through my successes. Sometimes Satan attempted to put me down through my failures. It whispered to my ears, "You failed" or "Give it up." Therefore, I was disappointed and desperate, because of being unaware of Satan's plot while I was in sleep. Pride and despair is Satan's twin weapon.

Look at those believers who contributed to human history. They did not depend on their own ability or wisdom but on God. Paul declared, "I can do everything through him who gives me strength" (Phil. 4:13) and "My message and my preaching were not with wise and persuasive words, but with a demonstration of the Spirit's power"(1 Cor. 2:4-5).

He testified that when he was weak, then he was strong because of presence of power of the Holy Spirit(2 Cor. 12:10).

There is a song written by Martin Luther, the great Reformer, titled "A Mighty Fortress is Our God", which we sing on Reformation Sunday. How he was courageous to challenge the Pope whom even kings feared, and began to reform with 95 Articles! Did he have a military corps? He must have failed according to human strategy. He had, however, a mighty power which was greater than tens of thousands of an elite troop. That power was described in the second stanza of the song.

> Did we in our own strength confide?
> Our striving world be losing

Were not right Man on our side
The Man of God own choosing
Dost ask who that may be?
Christ Jesus, it is He
Lord Sabaoth is His name
From and to age the same
And he must with the battle

When we are in spiritual sleep, we lose the glorious light from our hearts

When we are awake, the glorious light of heaven fills us up, so we are not shaken by the world glory. The hope of glory of the future in our hearts is like nuclear weapon, winning against Satan. Even when we are misunderstood, suffered, and persecuted for the sake of the Lord we could cry out like Stephen did, "Look, I see heaven open and the Son of Man standing at the right hand of God"(Acts. 7:56), for we have the glory of heaven in our hearts. We will be able to bear the cross silently just as the Lord did.

The reason we cannot overcome even small temptation is because we see only light of the world and are fascinated by it. The heaven's glory is like, gold, silver, and gems, while the world's glory is like ice cream. Bodily glory is like a flower ; it will be disappeared soon, but heavenly glory in our spirit is forever. We our spiritual eyes are open, how could we hurt our Lord by seeking world's glory? I once visited one of the churches for blind people in Korea. The senior pastor was also blind, and he was a powerful servant of God, filled with the Holy Spirit. He said,

"Churches today, are like the blind." If we call contemporary church blind church, would that be exaggerating?

Wake Up and Lift Heads Up!

We discussed above those spiritual phenomena when we are in spiritual sleep. The basic reason for our failures and disobedience to the word of God is because we are in sleep. The Bible, therefore, gives us warnings about the consequences of the sleeping.

Samson ended up his life miserably because he was sleeping on the lap of Delilah, being taken off his eyes by the Philistine. Jonah suffered in a big fish's belly for three days because he was trying to escape from God's mission, sleeping in a boat away from God. Peter was in sleep on Gethsemane instead of praying, and later he lost his temper and cut Margo's ear. He also denied Jesus three times after that. Eutychus fell from the upper room while he was in sleep. These are all warnings about spiritual sleep, not physical sleep.

We are living in a critical period of entire human history. As we have discussed above, Biblical prophecies about the signs of the Second Coming have been fulfilled for the last ten years or so. The last chance will be given to us. We should wake up and lift our heads up, and should listen to the final commission of our Lord.

God's Methods of Waking Us Up

God uses two methods to wake us up.

Through prophets or his servants

The Israelites were a special people whom God had chosen and loved to prepare for the first coming of Jesus. Whenever they were in spiritual sleep betraying God and worshipping idols, God woke them up and warned them through prophets. The mission of the prophets of the Old Testament was to deliver God's message and warn them even though the Israelites did not want to hear. They always delivered God's message by saying, "Thus says the Lord." There were always two responses to God's warnings. One was to repent and return to God, and the other was to become hardhearted and not to listen to him. When they listened to and returned to him, God had mercy and grace on them and forgave them, and blessed them in order to follow the mission. If they did not repent, God used a rod to wake them up.

I recently read a book, "America's Last Call" by David Wilkerson and guessed that there is still a prophet warning America. He strongly insists that America's prosperity is from God's last mercy and that if they do not repent there would be disaster in America, which is God's way of controlling human history. He quotes prophets' messages of the Old Testament who warned people and says that it is the same warning to America. He probably was weeping while he was writing, thinking about tears of the prophets. Does he overemphasize the current situation of America? He writes the following:

Federal courts are doing everything within their power to outlaw even the mention of God's name in public life. Judges are banning the symbols of faith left and right—crosses, religious pledges, manger scenes, and prayer in schools. And now a movement to remove the phrase "In God We Trust" from our coins is gaining popularity.

We are in an ocean of bloodshed, as we continue to allow the murder of millions of unborn children. Doctors are suctioning out the brains of fully developed babies in their first trimester. And nurses who unashamedly assist in abortions march in protest against killing of whales, minks, and rabbits. What arrogant hypocrites!

There is more than 100 million TV sets and some 100,000-movie theaters in America today—and most are serving as conduct for pornography! Sadly, few movies today can make money without an R rating. Even Disney movies and other family films promote cursing and occult, even among children. In fact, it has become popular to curse Christ with disdain—mocking him, ridiculing him, and dragging his name into the gutters of sensuality and violence.

Violence in America today has far surpassed that of the days in Noah or Lot. Almost every town, village and city in this country has experienced the shock of senseless murders. As a result, many people have literally locked themselves into their homes, afraid to walk the streets. Most Americans are dumb founded by all the senseless killings, especially among students. Our schools are now unsafe(p. 10).

Reading Wilkerson's book, I thanked God for sending a person like him to America who sadly warns us of the current situation.

Was there any other time in America's history more corrupted than today? Like Wilkerson views, is morality better now than Sodom and Gomorrah? There they surely practiced homosexuality in Sodom and Gomorrah, but did they legislate (make it legal) it like the state of Montana? There were gangs in Sodom and Gomorrah, but I doubt that they came into churches or schools killing innocent students or congregations. They did commit acts of lewdness for sure, but did they kill millions of embryos per year? This is tragic reality of America who boasts she is the only superpower in the world. Therefore, how can we say that Wilkerson is wrong? Some might make excuses that these symptoms are common throughout the world, but surely the reality of America today is darker than that of Sodom and Gomorrah.

The biggest problem in America, however, is the church itself. Jesus named the church "the light of the world." About 3 percent of ocean water is salt, and it is that amount of salt that prohibits ocean water from becoming foul. The corruption of society might be a natural result, because the Holy Spirit is not engaged in it but Satan is controlling it. There is no place that is not corrupted if Satan is in control. Who can reform this corrupted society? Politicians? University Professors? Scientists in labs? And Businessmen? No! It is the church's responsibility that has the mission of being the salt of the world. The biggest tragedy in America is that the salt does not play its role:rather it has become rotten all together. The most serious problem is that the church that lost its light in the dark world. The tragedy of the tragedies is the church that lost its conscience and dried up its tears of repentance without knowing its mission. Those who open their spiritual ears should wake up and lift their heads up hearing the crying of those that are attacked by Satan and have fallen down.

This rich land of America originally belonged to the American Indians. The reason God gave us this land of America was and is to serve him with fear, just like the Puritans did and accomplish his mission for us. In spite of the blessing where is America flowing today? We need to think about that.

If we are not listening to the prophets, he wakes us up with whipping

When the Israelites became hardhearted and did not listen to the prophets, sleeping, being away from God and being proud, God woke them with a whipping. This is the principle history of Israel and of God's involvement in human history. The whip of God was seen in various ways:famine, epidemic, war, and pulling out of a king's eyes and exiling of all his people. Sometimes we think lightly of prophets' warnings, so we have whipping from God. It applies in the same as way to an individual, family, society, nation or church.

The USA has been the only superpower since the victories of World War I and II and the Cold War. Economically, the US has broken the anticipations of scholars and the precedent records, and has continually developed for the past ten years. The government has a surplus from tax income revenue. It seems not that the US has any hypothetical rivals in economy, science, and military power and that she seems still the only superpower in the twenty-first century. If she, however, ignores God's warnings toward this age, she will have a tragic end before God's holy and just judgment on history.

Though the US participated in the World War II, she was not damaged too badly except at Pearl Harbor, Hawaii. After the War the US economy developed rapidly, becoming the first creditor nation in the world. Nobody anticipated that the US would become a debtor nation at that time. In fact, until 1973 the US was a creditor nation. After the energy crisis in 1973 and Vietnam War, the US has been indebted. She is still indebted. We should not forget from the experience of 1973 that if God whips, the US economy might collapse. Instead of being proud of today's prosperity, the US should return to God and use her prosperity for international missions and helping the poor. Isn't it the Christians who know much about the God's judgment of history? Where will she flow, if the Christians are in sleep?

We should not be proud of our military power. No one can exceed the US military power in the world. The US has the most recent scientific weapons. In the Vietnam War, however, the US was defeated. As I mentioned in the previous chapter, the future enemies must attack the US through guerrilla tactics. From the lessons of Vietnam and Afghanistan, any up-to-date scientific weapons or even the greatest power could not but fail before guerrillas' desperate contention under strong nationalism. They did

not know what to do even when the US embassies were destroyed
and staffs were held captivate. Only Christians know that the labor
of guards was useless if God does not protect. We Christians are
the guards of the US:if we are in sleep, where can these people
go? Wilkerson writes:

> A cartoon appeared in a New City Newspaper picturing the Titanic
> leaving port. The ship was renamed the US economy. The captain
> above read "not even God can sink this ship ⋯ The American dream
> is going to turn into the American nightmare. It will occur suddenly"
> without warning−and no one will be sellers only−no buyers−a
> majority of American has concluded, that morals do not count. Let
> our leaders do as they please ; just give us a booming economy.
> Let the good times roll. All that matters is prosperity.

If the Christians do not wake up now, there will be a fearful
judgment of history.

Foolish Christians usually wake up and return to God with tears
after being whipped by God.

When I visited Russia I met some university students who were
attracted by the American lifestyle. They were like me when I
was attracted by America after the World War Ⅱ. In the hotel
room on that night I looked back 30 years ago when I came to
the USA for the first time, and hoped that they would not come.
My yearning for life in America was beyond expression when
I first came to the USA because I was told by missionaries that
more than 85 percents of the whole population were Christians.

I imagined that America would be a "small kingdom of God" and I longed to see her, the earthly kingdom, established by the Puritans. When I arrived San Francisco International Airport it was breathtaking and fantastic, so I thought she was surely an earthly kingdom.

I went to Los Angeles to study at Fuller Seminary:it was winter with palm trees and beautiful flowers. One of my friends invited me to a welcome party, so I went by bus. I got off the bus, and walked the street toward my friend's between Vermont Ave. All of a sudden, some people threw me to a narrow side street. I turned to them, and there were three African Americans, pointing guns at me and saying, "Raise your hands. Close your eyes if you want to live." I closed my eyes and raised my hands, thinking that I would die today and asking God for help. They took my wristwatch, wedding ring, and cash form my wallet, and ran away. I was horrified, and finally managed to get my friend's house.

I never forget what my friend told me on that day:

> The USA is one of the two superpowers with the Soviet Union, but she has suffered from moral corruption. The US does not have a rival in the criminal ratio, divorce rate, drug and alcohol addiction. These are natural occurring event here and abroad. All the historical imperialists such as in Greece, Rome, Spain, France, and England were all ruined. The time when they became strong, they did not know they would be ruined, but they did. America could be ruined someday just as they did. Moral corruption of America today can be a proof of impending fall. When a country becomes a powerful

nation with prosperity, wealth, and power, it becomes proud and extravagant seeking enjoyment, especially sexual pleasure. The peak of sexual corruption is homosexuality. Even a huge and strong tree will be fallen by a breeze if a small worm is eating it up.

Today, America is walking toward the same road that those imperial countries had gone. There is strong possibility of ruin if they do not reform. American is a country built upon fear of God by the Puritans who loved freedom, justice, and peace. America's prosperity today is the fruit of their ancestors' planting. Most Americans today, however, do not fear God:instead they worship money and pleasure. They have to repent and return to God. The incidence you had this afternoon is rare in Korea or other countries in Asia, but it is everyday life in here, America. It is proven daily in the newspapers. Americans have become mentally numb because they have homicidal criminal actions every day. They live with it. It is a phenomenon of the end of the century, which is very sad. If the USA is destroyed first, then the atheistic tyranny of the Soviet Union will be in control all over the world. It is abomination. Far better, the Soviet Union should fall first.

He looked very sad when he talked about this.

God wakes us up with the revival of the Holy Spirit

"Then I saw another angel coming up from the east, having the seal of living God. He called out in a loud voice to the four angels who had been given power to harm the land and the sea:Do not harm the land or the sea or the trees until we put a seal on the foreheads of the servants of our God"(Rev. 7:2-3).

I briefly described above that the seven symptoms of spiritual sleep and how God wakes those who are in sleep. How can we be awake in this critical time? My own effort is not enough. When we are in a deep sleep even physically we need help to be awake. Spiritual sleep too needs the Holy Spirit's help to be awakened. If the Holy Spirit is present within me and wakes me up, then we can be awake, lifting our heads up to the work of God. Today, the Holy Spirit wakes us up through the prophecies of the book of Revelation just like an alarm clock.

There is the most surprising news to the churches of the end of the world. It is the promise of the revival in Revelation 7:2-3 as I quoted above. It must be a promise of the pouring out the Holy Spirit. Peter, when he preached on the Pentecost after he experienced the Holy Spirit, quoted Joel 2:28-32 in his sermon:

> In the last days, God says,
> I will pour out my Spirit on all people,
> Your sons and daughters will prophesy,
> Your young men will see the vision,
> Your old men will dream
> Even on my servants, both men and women,
> I will pour out my Spirit in those days,
> And they will prophesy(Acts 2:17-18)

This must be a promise of revival at the end of times.

Text Interpretation

Another Angel

The four angels in 7:1 were strong enough to hold back winds. Those angels, as described above, can be interpreted as the four superpowers that brought the age of the Cold War. The "another angel" infers just a regular country, not the superpowers.

God does His works in human history by choosing a certain nation or people. In the Old Testament era, God chose Israel, the descendant of Abraham in order to prepare the first coming of Jesus. The small Jewish community established the early church and started the world wide mission movement. In Middle Ages, however, God used Rome, in the 1800s England, and in the twentieth century he chose America and blessed her to continue the world mission.

From the East

This phrase can be interpreted as three different ideas:

1. From the east means from God. It can be inferred that a revival comes from God at the end of age.
2. It could be the eastern countries. God would bring a revival from the Far East.
3. Or, it could be a nation from Far East.

It is not necessary to argue which one is an appropriate interpretation among three. Wherever it comes from, Far East, South America, or Africa, the flame of revival will be spread out to the world. The first and most important task is to believe the promise of revival and wait for it repenting, yearning, and praying for its coming. Second, we should evangelize the unreachable that have never listened to the Gospel, recognizing God's promise and his provision for human history. This promise will be kept for those who believe and pray for it.

When the Revival Comes

When I was a graduate student at Fuller Theological Seminary I was taught by Dr. J. Edwin Orr who had studied the world history of revivalism. He taught a course named "The Awakening Movement." He summarized the characteristics of revivalism:

1. Revival is God's special grace and his gift like pouring out water.
2. Any specific local church, denomination, or region cannot limit the revival ; once the revival occurs, it spreads out to the world.
3. When the revival comes, it accompanies strong and fervent prayers. The relationship with God becomes closer and people stay up, worshipping, praising, and praying.
4. When one experiences the revival, he or she easily overcomes the world with strong power. Thus, the life of saints becomes holy.
5. Revival brings spiritual power to church and the individual. Revival helps us bear our own cross and overcome our own desires, sacrificing ourselves to help others. The revival movement led by John Wesley became the motivating force to overcome

the crises caused by the Industrial Revolution in England.

6. Revival will burn fires of the Holy Spirit for having compassion for the lost souls:people start evangelizing and churches are growing. Church becomes a mission center.

7. The result of the revival continues by an awakening movement for both people and church(From Dr. Orr's lecture notes).

Dr. Orr's research of the characteristics and its result of revival is proven from the Bible and from the testimonies of those who experienced a revival. The disciples of Jesus were scared after watching their master's death on the cross, locking the door (John 20). After they witnessed resurrection of Jesus with their own eyes, yet they acted the same. They, however, listened to Jesus' command, "Do not leave Jerusalem··· But you will receive power when the Holy Spirit comes on you ; and you will be my witnesses in Jerusalem, Judea, Samaria, and to the ends of the earth"(Acts 1:4-8). About 120 people gathered together at that upper room in Jerusalem and prayed fervently for about 10 days. At last, they had a great revival of the Holy Spirit on the Pentecost. That was the same phenomena as Orr's research results.

Luke, after experiencing the revival of the Jerusalem church wrote:

"They devoted themselves to the apostles' teaching and to fellowship, to the breaking of bread and to prayer. Everyone was filled with awe, and the apostles did many wonders and miraculous signs. All the believers were together and had everything in common.

Selling their possessions and goods, they gave to anyone as had need. Every day they continued to meet together in the temple courts. They broke bread in their homes and ate together with glad and sincere hearts, praising God and enjoying the favor of all people. And the Lord added to their numbers daily those who were being saved"(Acts 2:42-47).

After that, God gave people revivals as gifts in Christian history and their testimonies were similar to Orr's research, too.

It seems not easy to understand a revival for those who have not experienced it. One day, I attended a denominational meeting and one of the speakers preached about the necessity of revival and suggested to pray for an American revival. One of the pastors asked a question, "We believe in Jesus as our Lord and Savior, and that is a precise proof of the work of the Holy Spirit. We are experiencing a revival of the Spirit. Why do we need another revival?" The speaker read Acts 2:42-47 and responded, "If we are living now like the Jerusalem church, your question is appropriate." Peter was a believer who made a confession of faith before Jesus at Caesarea Philippi, but he did not experience the Holy Spirit until Pentecost. Another pastor asked, "The Holy Spirit on the Pentecost was a special and one time event that opened the age of the Holy Spirit. Does repetition of a revival come from the misinterpretation of the Bible?" The speaker read Acts 11:15, which shows what happened with Peter and the gatherings at Cornelio's:"As I began to speak, the Holy Spirit came on them as he had come on us at the beginning. Then I remembered what the Lord had said:'John baptized in water, but you will be baptized with the fire of the Holy Spirit.'"

We know the history of Christianity from the early church revival that there have been numerous revivals. Revival awakes people who are in sleep, revitalizing the church so that it may continue its mission. It was impossible for England world mission movement in 1800s without John Wesley's revival, and Korean church today without revival in 1907-8.

Korean Church Revival and Awakening Movement

Revival in 1956

In Korean church history there were two great revivals in 1907 and 1927. I will, however, discuss those revivals after the World War Ⅱ, which I experienced. The first revival that I experienced was in 1946. When Japan surrendered at discretion and Korea was liberated, Koreans who escaped from Japanese militarism to China, the Soviet Union, or the USA started coming back home. There were many Christians among them, including ministers and leaders. Another tragedy started when the powers which won the war decided to divide Korea into the South and the North according to the Yalta Agreement. They started a military administration by the US Army in the South and the Soviet Union Army in the North.

There were many people who came back from Manchuria in the North, and among them there was a minister named Sung Bong Lee. Churches in the North started having revival meetings, inviting Rev. Lee as a speaker. An amazing awakening movement and works of the Holy Spirit overwhelmed churches in the North. It was spread all over the areas. I walked for four hours to the place where he led a revival in Kang Dong, Pyung Ahn Nam Do. The church, which could accommodate about 300 people, was packed with much more people, having no place to sit. It was cold winter in February and there were even people who could not go into the church but stood outside listening through a megaphone.

The Holy Spirit started a revival work through Rev. Lee at that time. People wept for repenting sins and for overwhelming joy and thanksgiving for knowing forgiveness of their sins, and they prayed with loud voices without ceasing. They gave their honest testimonies and praise with tears. Some alcoholics and gang members attended and repented, becoming a new person. There were also the sick and those captured by evil spirits, and they were miraculously healed and delivered by the grace of God. Everybody experienced the presence of the Lord, and worshipped Him with awe. I was one of them. After the meeting was finished in the evening, people seemed to forget going back home and continued to sing and praise, repent and develop a strong conviction of faith, to share their testimonies and visions for commissions all night long.

This amazing flame of revival was spread out. It started with a few people, but the Holy Spirit's work of strong revival and great awakening was spread out to the entire church. Broken families were reunited, old debts were paid up, and all the wrong doings were confessed and forgiven. A thief surrendered voluntarily to the police, and other believers also turned from old habits and came to live a new way of living. Watching them changed through the works of God, non-believers started coming to church.

I also experienced revival, led by the Holy Spirit, and repented all my faults of the past. I apologized to an old enemy, and later he became a Christian and then committed himself to Christ by being a minister. I remembered the mistake that I made when I was 14 years old:I went to Pyung Yang by train. I told a lie to the ticketing employee that I was 12 years old, getting a half price. After the revival, I went to see the stationmaster and paid the half price back. The Buddhist stationmaster was impressed by my act and became a Christian later. I also remembered that I cheated on the graduation exam when I was in the 6th grade at the elementary school. I went to see my homeroom teacher confessing my fault, and he forgave me. After that, the atheist teacher believed in Jesus and was saved.

After the revival, those kinds of wakening movements took place in many places, giving praise to God. The number of believers had increased daily, and accordingly, the church had grown rapidly. They had Early Morning Prayer service in the church every morning and they were eager to meet even on Sunday evenings,

Wednesday evenings, and Friday evenings praising God and praying. In each home they started having family worship and prayers. The spiritual awakening movement also impacted society. After the communist government was established in the North, however, they started persecuting the Christians. As persecution became severe many Christian leaders crossed the 38th parallel, moving to the South. During the Korean War most Christians in the North escaped to the South, seeking religious freedom.

Revival in 1957

The second revival that I experienced was at the minister's mountain prayer meeting in August 1957. After the Korean War, Korea had a big project to rebuild the ruined country. There were about one million orphans on the street and about three hundred thousand widows with their young children, worrying about how they were going to live. At that time, Korea was managed with help and support from the USA. The Korean government was seriously corrupted, so the people criticized it. It was a dark period without hope for the future. In the midst of that, about 400 ministers from all over the nation gathered at Je Il Prayer Garden on Sam Kak mountain to pray for the nation and people.

It began on Monday evening and lasted until Friday evening. Speakers were not invited, yet senior pastors of local churches rotated delivering sermons for each meeting. They met three times a day for worship together:at 5:00-6:00 in the early morning, 10:00-12:00 in the morning, and 8:00-10:00 in the evening. It was very hot without air-conditioning, but we all praised God and prayed fervently. The chairman asked me to lead singing, so I did for each meeting. I was 29 years old at that time. After morning worship we found places under the trees, sitting down as groups, talking and resting. We had never had a vacation before, but we spent this prayer conference as if we had a vacation.

It was Wednesday morning around 10 o'clock. I was leading singing, and felt something different spiritually. We were singing hymns of "the sufferings of cross." Many had tears in their eyes, and some were weeping. We finally sang "Old Rugged Cross", and were all inspired by the Holy Spirit. We felt we were standing on Calvary, facing the suffering Lord. The preacher stood up and read Genesis 42 and said, "The brothers of Joseph were heading to Egypt with empty sacks. If they returned home without food, Jacob's families would starve to death. If they went back home with food, they would all be saved. Our people today are in crisis like Jacob's families were. We are the scapegoat of the war between the US and the Soviet Union. One million orphans are wandering on the ruined city streets, and three hundred thousand widows are weeping. Money and power, however, corrupt the statesmen. We smell corruption. God calls us light and salt in the world. The problem issues. Are our spiritual sacks not empty? If we are filled with the Holy Spirit, like Joseph's brothers filled their sacks with grains God will sustain and revive our people even though they are like dried bones of the Agor Valley. Let us repent."

When he finished, one minister started crying and screaming. He sat about 5 meters away from the pulpit. He was too loud to understand. I sat on the stage, so I was able to look at him directly. I thought he was a schizophrenic. All of a sudden, a surprising thing happened:starting with him, all of us started repenting and crying one by one. It was like ripped crops falling down by wind.

The speaker stopped preaching, and the Holy Spirit began to lead us. It was like relay praying:one after another, we continually prayed. One after another we gave our testimonies. Giving testimonies, we confessed that we were like false teachers, resounding gongs without love. We cried and blamed ourselves for our nation's tragedies.

The meeting lasted without ending. It was noon, but nobody left for lunch. Until the time for evening worship we were praying, repenting, singing, and giving testimonies. Tears covered everybody's face. From that morning until Saturday morning, the end of the meeting, the mountain was shaking with fervent prayers of the ministers. Nobody talked to each other or played chess game, but prayed or read the Bible. I was one of them, too. For the first time, I prayed for eight hours without stopping. I came to know on that day the meaning that praying by the Holy Spirit is unlimited by time or space.

Because this "Sam Kak Mountain" revival occurred among the ministers, it was rapidly spread out to the churches all over the country. A Prayer Movement took place:people started praying fervently very early in the morning, Friday overnight, and fasting and praying. I have seen abundant evidences of a revival's power:singings with great joy, burning with fires of saving souls, helping with love, and obedience and commitment, especially, there were many young people who committed their lives to the Lord. The revival and awakening brought Korean churches an enormous growth until the early 1970s. In 1965, Hwal Lan Kim led a national evangelism movement, which grew up to the world mission movement in the early 1970s. Today, the Korean church sends missionaries to almost every nation in the world.

Revival in 1962

The revival was expanded to the local churches. In 1962, the church where I served started having revivals. The church was located at Daeheung Dong, Deajeon where a strong Buddhist community was formed. In 1961, an individual, Jae Kook Park built the church and I was invited as the senior pastor. It was very hard to evangelize people, for almost of all them, even the leaders of the community, were Buddhists. After the Korean War the city was ruined and did not have enough food. Poor families could not afford to send their children to school. We began to teach children from poor families and we taught the youth who could not afford to go to middle school the Bible and other subjects at night. Of course, our ultimate goal was to evangelize the community through education.

As we started an educational ministry, the community leaders began to show their interest in our church and thank us. The mayor visited the church and gave thanks. Even though there was no education for children in the community this was a great problem, the government itself could do not because of lack of budgeting. There was a Buddhist temple in that community, but Buddhist leaders did not concern themselves with social issues. We also taught English and the Bible to elementary, middle school, and high school students on Saturdays. It was a tool for evangelizing the community.

After one year, we had about 45 students who attended Saturday school regularly. We took those students to a summer camp at Gye Ryong Mountain. It was very exciting for the students, because they had never had a vacation. There was no camp ground, so we took three tents:one for the girls, one for the boys and one for the staff and for a place for worship. My only prayer was that they would experience the Holy Spirit so that they might become new persons and commit themselves to Jesus Christ. We taught the Bible in the morning, games and plays in the afternoon, worship in the evening, and we let them pray individually after the worship.

It was Wednesday night. After the evening worship, we let the students out to pray for 30 minutes. When 15 minutes passed, however, we had a shower. I rang the bell to bring them inside the tent. I counted students, but two boys did not come back. I went to out to search for them, calling out their names loudly. About three minutes later, they were walking back in rain, singing hymns. Their voice sounded like that of the Holy Spirit.

Other students went back to their tents. The two boys continued to pray, repenting their sins. The Holy Spirit started moving. Other students who went back to their tents came back to know what was happening. After a while, everybody was there. One of the two boys stood up and began to talk. He said that though he was attending the church, he disobeyed to his parents, cheated on exams, smoked, drank, lied, and wanted to meet girls at church, and he asked us to forgive, crying and weeping. At that moment, the fires of revival started burning in everybody's heart. Every student knelt down to the Lord and repented their sins. I prayed and asked the Holy Spirit to lead them. On that night, we stayed up until dawn, praying, singing, and giving testimonies with teardrops.

From the next day, there was a big change. Those who complained about games being too short sat under the trees, reading the Bible even during the breaks. Two or three students sat around talked about only what they found about faith and about themselves and how they felt. There was a "fellowship of the saints" written in the Acts. On the Saturday morning, on the way back, they were still singing hymns on top of the truck.

We arrived at church. After arrival worship, we dismissed them. I came back home and was preparing a sermon for Sunday. Then two policemen came to me and said that they had a report that some people came into the church with weapons. They needed my permission to go into the church. I was astonished, so went to the church with the policemen. We found that the students did not go home, but they gathered at the prayer room in the basement. They were praying fervently for their parents' salvation, pounding the wooden floor with their hands. The sound of 45 students' praying and pounding was like a big fight, so the neighbor reported to the police. The policemen laughed and went back, I glorified God for those students who prayed for their families. As the result of the revival, the students' life had been changed and their Buddhist parents began to realize that Jesus was the true God through their children's new life, and began to start converting. The fire of revival started burning among the high school students and expanded to the adults. The church began to grow as a church of praying and evangelizing. About four years after the revival, the Buddhist community changed as Christian community, and our church membership grew up to 2,000 from 150. Every Sunday, we had new members between 5 and 10. I even could not remember each person very well. We had to rebuild the church building.

In America, they call a mega-church if the membership is over 5,000. In Korea, however, the same membership is regarded as mid-size. The largest congregations of every denomination such as Presbyterian, Baptist, Methodist, and Assembly of God are in Korea. Among the Third World church, Korea is the only country that sent more than 10,000 missionaries throughout world. I think all these are results of revival. I earnestly hope that there would be a kind of revival in America, too.

The Lord says, "Do not cry for me, but cry for your children."

The Lord seeks for those who cry for the tragic reality of America, corrupted like Sodom and Gomorrah.

Revival and the Final Mission

I previously reminded that the prophecies about the Second Coming of Jesus, Israel's independence, and independence movement of the weak and small nations have been fulfilled recently, around 1988 when the age of supra-Cold War came. One prophecy has not been fulfilled yet:Matthew 24:14.

"And this gospel of the kingdom will be preached in the world as a testimony to all nations, and then the end will come."

There are still ethnic groups who have never heard the Gospel. The experts in mission report that there are about 2,000 ethnic groups left within the 10-40 Window. Our final mission is to wake up and make our best effort to fulfill the word.

Christians in Mission

"As the Father sent me, I am sending you"(John 20:21). Our Lord was sent by God and gave his life to save us. The Lord redeemed us with his blood, making us his own, and then sends us in the world. The original meaning of the word "to send" is the same as "missionary." Therefore, he sends us all. We give ourselves as living sacrifices just as he did so that we may accomplish the mission that he has given us to win the souls.

Some of us are sent missionaries who go to the mission field to preach the Gospel, and others are sending missionaries who are in charge of prayers and supplies. Christians who are not missionaries are not real Christians. Those who live by the principle of mission are missionaries whether they are in mission fields or not. I call this "missionarization" or "mission consciousness."

People who have been missionarized live for the purpose of mission. Whether they are in businesses or work for a company or whether they are farmers, students or getting married they have to offer themselves as living sacrifices to the throne of the Lord, committing their lives as missionaries. Making money cannot be a purpose, but doing missions is with the money that they have earned.

Lifestyle of Missionarized Christians

Those who perceive themselves as missionaries should live by the lifestyle of missionaries.

1. Pray for the missionaries on a daily basis. Praying for the missionaries is like backup shooting at war. Our prayers are always answered and give missionaries strength. When they have difficulties, we should pray and fast for them.

2. Give tithes and mission offerings. Our duty is to support missionaries. If they are out of bullets, it is impossible to continue a war. Giving offerings regularly is very important

to meet missionary's needs.

3. Live a plain life. Missionarized Christians should live a simple and plain life as missionaries do. To do that, Christians should practice frugality and save to support mission. I was missionarized in 1975. I served as a director of a mission organization. I took an official trip to Africa for the first time. I saw different things, but I cannot forget two things. One was African poverty and the other was the life the western missionaries who lived plain life under the heat, giving up convenient life. I was so ashamed. I repented with tears because my life was extravagant and not controlled.

After I came back home I showed my family how the Africans lived a primitive life on slide. We discussed how we could help those who worked for the Africans and the ways that we could save some money to support the missionaries. The following was our decision on that night:

1) Do not go to the barbers. Trim our hair at home, and the money goes to the mission offering.
2) Do not trade in cars. Use them until out of service. Saving money goes to the mission offering.
3) Only one suit for each season. Saving money goes to the mission offering.
4) Try not to go the beauty shop (for my wife) too often.

The next day, I bought hair-trim kit, and my wife trimmed my hair for the first time. My hairstyle was like that of an acorn. I felt embarrassed a little, but I encouraged myself to preach the next Sunday, thinking about the missionaries under that strong heat.

The problem was that the lady choir members could not sing but laugh after seeing my hairstyle behind me. I had to explain to the congregation. People became quiet and nobody laughed. I have never been to the barbers after that. I have tried to live plainly like a missionary, but it has not been easy. One surprising fact is that I am not ashamed of using an old car now, which I was before. I am proud of that. Hallelujah!

Missionarized Christians will not be proud of luxurious cars, furniture, clothes or accessories. Their lives are plain and simple, and give abundantly to missions for the Gospel. Ministers and congregation are willing to sacrifice for mission. They declare, "Our present sufferings are not worth comparing with the glory that will be revealed in us." Then, they will rejoice like the pearl merchant who rejoiced after purchasing a valuable pearl. It is amazing grace that we can participate in the sufferings of our Lord, and that we take parts in his mission. I was told that the parents of President Bush's chauffeur were proud of their son's job.

That makes sense. How about us? Are we not commissioned by Christ the King to do his mission? It is up to the last runner to win a relay. We are like the last runners of history. The previous runners did their best, even bleeding. Some of them became food for hungry lions at Colosseum in Rome, and others ran to the point of death by sword. We have a great responsibility, running the final round. Let us run best so that all of Jericho shall fall.

Becoming Immune to the Second Coming

The theory of impending Second Coming has been spread out from the early church, so it seems that it became immune for the contemporary Christians. Some mystics prophesied recently the date of the Second Coming and deluded Christians. The basis of our faith is only the Bible. We do not believe in the image of Jesus in our dreams or visions. Nor believe in debate after theories or reasons. Think about the historical figures. We believe in president Washington through historical records and writings. The only basis of our faith in Jesus is the word of God. Especially, the Gospels are records of historians, like Luke and other disciples that followed Jesus and listen and watch what he said and what he did in his contemporary.

We do not believe Jesus' Second Coming through visions or other sources. We believe prophesies in the Bible, especially, the books of Gospels and the book of Revelation. Because they did not have a written Bible in the early church, they believed his promise to come again. After the canonization of the Bible, however, we need to watch and wait carefully for the fulfilling the prophecy of the Second Coming.

I have tried to prove historically that the biblical prophecy of Jesus' Second Coming is faithful, and that almost all the prophecies have been fulfilled in our times. In the near future, he will come again with chief angels' trumpet, and the lost Garden of Eden will be restored. Let us wake up and lift our heads up. Let us accomplish the final task on the great commission, being like the wise five girls, not the foolish ones.

The Bibliography

Books in Korean

이상근 박사의 계시록 주석

박윤선 박사의 계시록 주석

김상복 목사의 계시록 강해

이병규 목사의 계시록 주석

김철손 박사의 계시록 강해

유형기 목사의 계시록 주석

정양수 목사의 계시록 강해 설교

고석희 목사의 제3세계 선교 전략

김춘배 목사의 한국교회 수난 사화

김광수 목사의 한국교회 수난사

곽안전 박사의 한국 교회사

민병배 박사의 한국 교회사

김광수 박사의 한국 기독교 100년사

김진환 목사의 한국교회 부흥 운동사

김영헌 목사의 한국 기독교사

김학수 박사의 세계기독교사

이희범 저, 유럽 통합론—EU정책과 대응전략
최영보, 이주선 김정배, 차상철, 박인숙, 박성심, 권오신, 김진웅 공
저, 미국 현대 외교사
영욕의 한국 경제 비사—경제기획원 33년
이원설 박사 저, 20세기 향한 비전과 리더쉽

Books in Japanese

石油の世紀(上·下)----------------翻譯--------------日本 放送 出版 協會
日本 市場 革命------------田坂 廣志 著---------東洋 經濟 新聞社
世界 經濟 Q=A----------------------------日本 經濟 新聞社 編
20 世紀 世界 時計--------高 野 孟 著---------集英社
20 世紀 戰爭史--------------松村 召 著---------PHP 研究所
文明の 大 轉換--------------沈野 一幸 著---------德門 書店
世界 經濟 大 不況 警告---三上 義一 譯-------甲川 書店
世界 經濟 動向------------竹村 件壹 著---------靑春 出版社
世界 經濟 恐慌--------------水野 隆德 著---------東洋 經濟 新聞社
歐洲 政治史------------------金丸 煇男 編--------有 裵 閣
情報 革命----------------------甲川 優 著----------法令 出版社
基督敎 史----------------------栢井 園 著----------新敎 出版社4.

Books in English

The Pulpit Commentary
The Calvin Commentary
The Great Bible Commentary edited by Disciples Publishing House

Revelation of John by William Barclay

Church Growth in Korea by Dr. Roy E. Shearer
A History of the Christian by William Walker
Fox's Book of Martyrs edited by Marie King
The History of Protestant Mission in Korea(1832-1910)
A History of Christian Mission by Stephen Neill
A History of Christianity by Kenneth S. Latourette
The Progress of Worldwide Missions by Rev. Robert Hall Glover
Understanding Church Growth by Dr. Donald McGavran
The Rise and Fall of the Great Nations, by Dr. Paul Kennedy
Progressing the 20 Century, by Dr. Paul Kennedy
Operation of the World, edited by Patrick Johnstone
The Clash of Civilizations, Making World Order, by Dr. Samuel Huntington
The Third Wave, by Alvin Toffer
The Prize, by Daniel Yergin
The Coming Economic Earthquake, by Larry Burkett
The Downing Street Years by Margaret Thatcher
The Last Giants, by George Otis Jr.
The Last Call to America, by Dr. Davit Wilkerson